FADO

OTHER WORKS BY ANDRZEJ STASIUK
IN ENGLISH TRANSLATION:

White Raven
Tales of Galicia
Nine

FADO

by Andrzej Stasiuk

Translated by Bill Johnston

Dalkey Archive Press
Champaign and London

First published by Wydawnictwo Czarne, Wołowiec, 2006
Copyright © Andrzej Stasiuk, 2006
Translation copyright © Bill Johnston, 2009
First English translation, 2009

Library of Congress Cataloging-in-Publication Data

Stasiuk, Andrzej, 1960-
 [Fado. English]
 Fado / Andrzej Stasiuk ; translated by Bill Johnston. -- 1st English translation.
   p. cm.
 Includes bibliographical references.
 ISBN 978-1-56478-559-6 (pbk. : alk. paper)
 1. Stasiuk, Andrzej, 1960---Travel--Europe, Central. 2. Europe, Central--Descrip-
tion and travel. 3. Cities and towns--Europe, Central. I. Johnston, Bill, 1960- II.
Title.
 PG7178.T28F3313 2009
 891.8'5803--dc22
 [B]
                              2009016734

Partially funded by a grant from the Illinois Arts Council, a state agency, and by the
University of Illinois at Urbana-Champaign

This publication has been subsidized by Instytut Książki – the ©POLAND Translation
Programme

www.dalkeyarchive.com

Cover: design and composition by Danielle Dutton; illustration by Nicholas Motte
Printed on permanent/durable acid-free paper and bound in the United States of
America

CONTENTS

Highway

Best of all is night in a foreign country. Come sunset you leave some place because it's turned out to be hopelessly boring, and you set out, let's say, due south. Darkness is descending onto the plains, covering up their melancholy, and by ten in the evening you're driving through pure black space. You can imagine all sorts of things to yourself; you can guess at the outline of the unseen landscape, the fields, orchards, the towns of white stone, the churches and squares cooling after the heat that lasted all day; you can try and come to terms with the perverse abundance of matter, the pornographic immodesty of history, which is lying on its back beyond every curve and over every hill; but ultimately it all turns out to be futile, because we remain alone with the space, which is the oldest of all things.

Road No. 4, road No. 1, road No. 13; red and white lights, lines on the asphalt stretching into infinity, mirages in the side mirrors, a glare that dissolves in the hot black air, intersections, green signs with place names, beltways and viaducts, tangles of asphalt ribbons around the beating hearts of cities, strings of trucks like vast railroad trains trailing skeins of foul-smelling shadow, demented will-o'-the-wisps in the fast lane going a hundred, a hundred-ten miles an hour, as if they were trying to drive all the way through the center of the night and reach the sunrise while others are still traveling in the dark . . . Yes indeed, the extreme solitude of the highway, where for hours on end you don't see a single living soul, only condensations of humanity with its obsessive need to be in motion and to get the better of infinity. Nothing but two-dimensional profiles, barely corporeal blurs behind the windshield, holding lit cigarettes or picking their noses. Unless you happen on a gas station, where everyone looks either like a weary potential victim or a restless sneak thief, while the immense blind bodies of long-haul trucks resemble huge boulders against the dark blue sky.

That's right, best of all is night in a foreign country on the highway, because at those times foreignness extends across the entire earth and sweeps everyone up indiscriminately in its flow. Somewhere on the horizon are the fires of human settlements, indistinguishable from the distant glimmer of the stars. Oh, the flickering artery of nothingness, oh, the recollection of ancient times when we were homeless in the world, when space was terrifying in its immensity. Now it irks us with its elusiveness.

After four hours I gave up. I couldn't be bothered to read the map. I took the first exit that came along and followed a narrow snaking road down into a tree-filled valley. Up above, the six-lane highway was raised on gigantic concrete piers. Headlights crisscrossed the sky, and a monotonous rumble drifted down like heavy dust. A few minutes later everything had vanished and fallen silent. I was driving through a forest. From time to time I passed buildings. They were dark. Everyone was asleep. I had no idea where I was. In the middle of the wooded wilderness I spotted a lone house with a lighted driveway. It was a bar. A thickset man in a white apron and a chef's hat was watching TV. In the semi-darkness the freshly washed floor shone; the legs of upturned chairs poked toward the ceiling. There were no customers. I asked for a glass of wine. He turned a silver-colored tap and poured without measuring. He said that unfortunately he couldn't offer anything to eat, that the kitchen was closed, but he could make me a sandwich. I didn't feel like eating. I explained that I wanted more wine. He found an empty liter bottle behind the bar and asked if that was enough. I nodded. He smiled and turned the tap again.

Half an hour later I drove off the road onto a track through the woods; I found a patch of grass, climbed into my sleeping bag, and after three mouthfuls of wine I fell asleep.

In the morning I set off in search of coffee. I passed isolated houses lost amid the green hills. Eventually I came to a town. Across from the café was a gas station. The three pumps stood right on the sidewalk. Four elderly men were sitting among them. They'd brought chairs from somewhere and were just sitting there. They were warming themselves in the morning sun, immobile as lizards. They were all smoking. Or rather, the cigarettes were burning down of their own accord in the men's hands. Columns of ash grew and then fell to the ground. Every so often a scooter would pull up and then one of the men would rise, pour gas, and take the money. I caught the mixed smell of gasoline and tobacco smoke. They were observing the street in silence, from under lowered eyelids. They didn't speak to one another, because they'd already seen everything in life and there was nothing to talk about. As the sun moved across the sky, the shadow cast by the overhang of the roof gradually approached their feet. This was their place and they knew that before the day heated up they would already be safe in a patch of coolness.

Afterwards I walked past them. From where they sat they could see over the roofs of the houses to the gray piers of the highway embedded in the dark green of the hills three or four miles away.

A Slavic *On the Road*

So then, all of this reminding myself, this sitting on my back-side in the semi-darkness and constantly traveling backwards, this staring into memory's rearview mirror, this lyric of loss, this Slavic *On the Road* that I'm knocking out on my type-writer—at three-fifteen A.M.—I'm going through it all not so as to remember, but so as to keep recalling everything from the beginning, to keep starting again from the beginning, un-til thought and illusion finally cover up reality, wipe it clean, erase all the names and landscapes and events, without which a person can do just fine, and the adventures that could just as easily have happened to someone else . . .

Because traveling is nothing. What's most important is what begins afterwards, right now, when everything's come to a stop, lost its nerve, and is slowly turning to nothingness. Five hours ago, at dusk, I was taking the hairpin bends of Šarišská Vrcho-vina and watching clouds gather over the central ridge of the Carpathian Mountains. In Klenov and Kvačany and Rokycany it was still light, it was light over Čerhov, but a lilac-colored darkness was already falling to the north. The only faint light came from a horizontal fissure somewhere between Lacková and Jaworzyna. After that, the sky's dark-blue eyelid closed shut for good, and as I was filling up in Prešov I saw the first veins of lightning. By the time I reached the border crossing in Becherov, I was already driving through the storm.

Now I'm sitting in the window and following it with my gaze. The thunder's out of earshot now, but over and again the rim of the hill flares up with a cold light. The clouds are moving due south. I imagine all the places I visited today. Flashes of lightning summon them from the darkness. People are asleep at home in their beds. Electric brightness bares their bodies. The Rusyns in Regetovka, the Slovaks in Lipany, the Gypsies in Zborov, the Hungarians in Silická—they all look the same: lying on their backs, rolled into a ball, on their sides, their mouths open. For a split second their faces look like silver masks, then they're returned to the darkness and once again become invisible. In their nightshirts, pajamas, long johns, or naked, alone or in pairs, apart or huddled together like animals, in separate rooms like the rich, in any case innocent and barely alive.

Is a sleeping person a Hungarian? Or a Gypsy? Is he a Pole? I take a mouthful of Kelt beer from its special bottle and I'm not at all sure. The storm is now passing over some part of Silická planina and in a moment it'll cross the Hungarian border like some kind of cosmopolitan utopia. It'll descend on Putnok, on Miskolc, and on the Bükk Mountains, and will continue moving south till it's extinguished by the dawn.

I once spent eight hours on the Ukrainian-Romanian border. It was nighttime. Our bus, filled with Ukrainian peddlers, just stood there. I sat on the curb, smoking and watching the dogs. They were totally devoid of any sense of statehood. A pack of them would burst out from behind the buildings on the Romanian side and disappear barking into Ukraine. They'd see off some of the departing cars and then come back. They formed platoons and defended their appointed areas. They snapped at one another, sniffed about, padded here and there, and time and again crossed the stretch of no-man's-land with its guardhouses. The border guards seemed not to notice them. If the dogs had wanted they could have set off on a canine expedition into the heart of the divided territories, crossing successive frontiers. For example, the Romanian-Bulgarian border, after that the Bulgarian-Yugoslavian, and then via Hungary and Slovakia they could have found themselves back in the same place, and no one would have stopped them. I was certain of it. At the crossing from Hungary to Romania in Petea I've seen their tribesfolk, and they're just as internationalist, just as crafty, and just as gaunt.

Meanwhile, the Romanians were disinfecting our bus. They were simply spraying the entire bodywork with some kind of fluid, as if the vehicle were tainted with the plague. Inside, Ukrainian women passed each other roast chicken legs and bread rolls and washed them down with beer. Then they looked at photos from someone's wedding. They looked like a single large family. The back of the bus was filled with goods. Bicycle wheels, inner tubes, tires, boxes of candy, bundles, crates of canned food, large packets of washing powder, and goodness knows what all else were piled up to the roof. The women sat there and waited till the amount of the bribe to be paid was reduced to a reasonable figure. Their calm fatalism was the equal of the dogs' freedom. It seemed that for them, the border—an abstract line dividing two rather similar territories—did not exist. They dozed or reminisced; they smelled a little of sour milk and a little of sawdust. They were sitting the way you do at home when there's no work to be done, or at the station when your train is running late.

All this comes back to me now as I sip my Kelt and watch the storm traveling south: the clouds like those vagrant dogs, like the bundles of the Ukrainian women, like the women themselves—bulky, patient, and sure of what they know. I imagine the women passing over my Europe encircled by a cumulus of those familiar red-and-blue checkered bags, as they float across barriers, laden with an assortment of necessities, as they move steadfastly like broad galleons, their skirts filling like sails, and drop to earth at the bazaar in Suceava, the Záhony marketplace, the Ten Year Stadium in Warsaw . . .

That's right. For some years now I've been oppressed by visions. I set off for the southern or the eastern border, I come back a week or two later, and I try to establish what actually happened and what was a fiction. Stray occurrences peep from behind the homogeneous material of the world. Time cracks and falls apart and, in order not to go mad, you have to continually recreate it. This fragility, this transitoriness, this impermanence of time is a characteristic of my part of the world. Time here never flowed in the steady, calm current found in the great metropolises. There was always something in its way. It divided, multiplied, twisted and turned back, entering into strange relations with space, at times becoming entirely still, then disappearing.

This summer we got lost in Romania. I took the wrong road in Satu Mare and instead of heading for the Hungarian border I turned southwest, toward Oradea. Road No. 19 was pretty deserted. The sun was blindingly low over the horizon. We'd already driven twelve hundred miles on the twisting roads of Maramureş and Bukovina and Transylvania and we were tired. We needed a rest from the madness of changing images and landscapes, we needed a break from all the unrelenting otherness. And then, from the other direction, from among the golden rays of the sun, from a light-filled void, there emerged a Gypsy caravan. The four wagons, drawn by four skinny horses, were roofed with tattered plastic sheeting. They were hung about with objects—buckets, tin cans, empty plastic oil canisters. We passed them, then without a word I shifted into reverse, while Piotr grabbed his Leica and slung his Nikon over his shoulder. I stayed in the car and he set off towards them. They simply stopped and waited. They were dark-skinned, ragged, colorful. They had nothing that in our eyes could be considered of any value. Blankets, pots, their archaic rickety vehicles, and animals that were as thin as they were. They'd taken a shortcut here from the depths of times long gone, and they felt perfectly comfortable in the present. With Piotr they negotiated a price for being photographed. They didn't want money, they wanted cigarettes. I handed over all the cigarettes I had in the car. They stood there patiently, smiling, the young women giving flirtatious looks. They'd come from long ago when people needed much less, and they were trying to live in the present, or rather they were allowing the present to flow past them; they probably regarded it as an element to be made use of, like fire for cooking or water for washing. The children approached the car; I gave out what was left of our candies, chips, snacks, whatever we had. I could see that they were treating me indifferently, pragmatically. The car, Piotr's cameras, our presence in general was for them an entirely natural phenomenon—in the sense of the natural world, which is there to be exploited. In a paradoxical way, they repaid beauty with beauty. We had reduced their humanity to an exotic image, they limited ours to the economy of their own survival.

It's night, rain is falling, and I recall all this for the umpteenth time. I recently re-read Ádám Bodor's *Sinistra Zone*. Bodor and his mythical Sinistra are superimposed transparently on the real Marmureş and Bukovina, while both are overlaid with the diaphanous living matter of my own thoughts, love, fear. Here, that is to say in Sinistra, everything belonged to the mountain sharpshooters, to Colonel Puiu Borcan, and later, after he died, to Izolda Mavrodin-Mahmudin, also a colonel, known as "Coca" for short. From the Baba Rotunda pass you could look down over Pop Ivan; below, narrow-gauge wood-fired locomotives would be crawling along. The inhabitants of Sinistra wore dog-tags round their necks. Any newcomer who tarried for a while received a new name. From time to time, outside Pop Ivan, Coca set up ambushes for Mustafa Mukker-man, who transported mutton in his truck from somewhere in Ukraine all the way to Thessaloniki or even Rhodes; along with the mutton, the refrigerated compartment sometimes also contained warmly dressed humans. Comrades from Po-land informed Coca of the plans being laid by Mukkerman, a six-hundred-and-fifty pound half-Turk, half-German. In these parts, watered-down denatured spirits were used to marinate dried mushrooms, and were drunk with a fermented juice made from wild berries. Frosted windows for the Sinistra prison were made by Gabriel Dunka in his shop: he placed sheets of glass in a chest filled with sand and walked over them barefoot for many hours. He was thirty-seven years old and a dwarf. One rainy day he took the naked Elvira Spiridon into his van and for the first time in his life experienced the scent of a woman's body. But loyalty got the better of desire and he turned her in, because it was only by chance she had not gotten into Mukkerman's truck instead.

Sinistra keeps me from sleep. Especially when it's raining. "Today, Central Europe is a concept that may only make sense to meteorologists" (Josef Kroutvor). So then, myth-making and meteorology . . . Though I can't figure out which of them has been troubling me more of late. Lined up on my shelf there are *The History of Ukraine*, *The History of Bulgaria*, *The History of Hungary*; there's a mass of other, lesser histories and stories, including *Slovakian History* and Eliade's *The Romanians*, but nothing comes of it. I read it all at bedtime and in the end I fall asleep, but I've never dreamed of John Hunyadi, or Czar Ferdinand, or Vasile Ursu Nicola—known as Horea—or Vlad the Impaler, or Father Hlinka, or Taras Shevchenko. At most I dream of the highly enigmatic Sinistra Zone. Of uniforms of nonexistent armies and ancient wars in which no one dies for real. I dream of white limestone ruins and mustachioed guards watching over borders on the other side of which everything changes and at the same time nothing changes at all. I dream of banknotes with the likenesses of heroes on one side and desolate windswept panoramas on the other. And I dream of small change too. And packets of cigarettes I've never smoked. I dream of gas stations on the plains, all of them resembling the one on the outskirts of Nové Mesto in Slovakia; and I dream of cans of Red Bull bearing the inscription: *špeciálne vyvinutý pre obdobie zvýšenej psychickej alebo fyzyckej namahy*. I dream of crumbling watchtowers amid bleak scenery, and cyclists wheeling their rusty bikes across a hilly country between towns whose names can be pronounced in at least three different languages; I dream of horse-drawn carts, and of people, and food, and hybrid landscapes and all the rest.

Yes indeed, rain is falling on all those places; it's raining on Maramureş, on dreams, on Sinistra; it rained on Spišské

Podhradie that day, Friday, July twenty-first, when we pulled up on a muddy parking lot by the Margecianka River. Single-story buildings lined the only street. We walked down the narrow sidewalk. We found a yellow-painted synagogue. It was crowned with four metal-plated domes. Its vaulted windows were black and dead. They looked as if they'd been transplanted from a nineteenth-century factory. In the gaps between the temple and the other buildings you could see hills and the distant towers of Spišská Kapitula. White ruins perched on the high ground overlooking the town. They were so large and bright they looked more like some kind of meteorological anomaly, an angular pile of cumulus clouds or a mirage transposed from a land that had long since ceased to exist. A car drove past, then another, and everything fell silent. The gray Škoda was disappearing into the green shade of the trees, but in reality it was vanishing in time. It moved through a tunnel dug out of the stillness. The road passed through the town as if through the center of a mountain, as if through backcountry, through a foreign territory that generously permitted transit. A fat, dark-skinned woman emerged from a squat house at a bend in the road and threw soapy water onto the asphalt, erasing all trace of the vehicles that had passed by. A little ways further, in a low open window I saw the interior of a large room. Someone had begun a job and quit half way through. Through the center of the room there ran a freshly built brick wall. A television was on somewhere in the depths of the house. A blue glow flashed and faded in the gloom. Alongside the new wall stood a pool table. Several balls lay there from an unfinished game. It was too dark for me to see their colors. I only caught the smell of quicklime and dry rot. Somewhere on the other side of the wall, of the darkness, of the chattering television, raised men's voices could be heard. Then I saw them in a narrow passage between the houses. They were arguing over an upturned stroller. One of them was turning the spoked rim of a wheel, while the other was shaking his head and gesticulating to say it was only good for scrap, that nothing could be done with it and they'd have to start over from the beginning. They were swarthy, thickset, animated, as if their bodies were immune to the motionlessness all around them, as if they existed in a different, weightless space. They probably did. They lived in a former Jewish neighborhood, on the outskirts of a Slovak town, at the foot of a Hungarian castle, and so in order to exist, in order not to disappear, they needed to establish their own rules, their own particular theory of relativity, their own law of gravity, which would keep them on the surface of the earth and prevent them from vanishing into the cosmic void, the abyss of memory.

We returned to the car and drove on. The stocky woman was once again coming out of her house with a bowl of suds. The Margecianka ran down below to the right. To the left rose the ridge of Drevenik. On its side were the Gypsies' houses, standing on terraces dug into the slope. These were not someone else's houses, dwellings from long ago inherited from others, but their own. They resembled children's drawings, they were so simple, small, and flimsy. They looked like ideas that had just begun to materialize. They were made of pine logs barely stripped of their bark—just poles really, no thicker than a man's arm—and covered with tar-papered gable roofs. They were so modest that the most a person could do was sit in them and wait out the time between one event and the next. They clung to one another, piling up like a wooden pueblo. Resinous smoke rose from their slender chimneys. There was a confusion of junk-filled yards; a living, disorderly substance composed of seemingly dead and used-up objects covered the earth like postindustrial foliage. It could just as easily have been the day they first arrived there as the day they were due to move on. Down below, children were playing along the shady road. The adults were standing talking about their own affairs, or maybe about the outsiders who drove through from time to time. Here everything belonged to them. I had no idea that space could be taken so unambiguously and irreversibly into possession, without causing it any harm. A little further on, all on her own, stood a young woman in a red dress. I seem to recall she was very beautiful. She was looking somewhere off to the side, where nothing was happening. I saw her for a split second, then the little red flame was extinguished in the rearview mirror.

Bulatović

They met on the broad exercise yard of the refugee camp in Zirndorf, after a bloody brawl in which the Poles and Hungarians emerged victorious, while the Czechs, Romanians, and Yugoslavians took a beating.

"If you hadn't pulled me aside, that Romanian would've put my eye out," said Kolar, embracing Marković.

"He ended up putting the Pole's eye out instead."

"What does a Pole need two eyes for!"

"Good point," said Kolar, laughing with him. "For a Pole even one eye is too much."

The Pole, an angular thirty-year-old, was covered in blood, on his knees howling. He was holding something in his outstretched hands. Marković had never seen an eye out of its socket. It was small, dead, devoid of any meaning, an émigré object.

Well all right, Yiddish isn't my mameloschn, *but I still know how to call "Haser enier!" I'll need another Cuban if you want me to say more. "You peasant bastard, I didn't rip your head off in Kiev but I'll tear your balls off in Munich!" says the Russian in his own language to the Ukrainian, and the Ukrainian answers in German: "You Russki pig, my gang'll be waiting for you across the Izara!" The Romanian mutters to himself: "My dear Popescu, Prince of the Balkans, perish with honor for king and monarchy!" The Bulgarian only opens his mouth when he's either eating or shitting, and after an argument about who the Danube belongs to, he strangles Prince Popescu without a word. "I'll get drunk and leave you all behind!" shouts the mad inebriated Pole, Dominik Kowalski, not letting anyone remove his knife from the Slovak's guts. The Czech, Flauta Pokorný, kneels and whimpers like a puppy dog, saying something about the White Mountain and Munich; he bites down on soap to keep from crying. "I'll pull the stars from the sky in your honor, o Hungaria!" moans the Hungarian, Árpád Nagy, in a hoarse, dreamy voice. There's no language into which anyone could translate what the Serb says to the Croatian, or what the Croatian replies to the Serb.*

Miodrag Bulatović never saw the realization of his dark dream. This can be read as either the malice or the kindness of fate. But it's also possible that, out of concern for his heart, fate preferred to find him a different occupation than that of writer, in a different world where good and evil are more evenly balanced, or simply immaterial. In any case, all these hypotheses indicate that he was a far from ordinary writer. A mediocre one would have been given the opportunity to watch the show all the way to the end, because it would be clear from the get-go that he would take sides and emerge from it all unscathed.

Today I find it hard to believe there was a time I read his books as engrossing fictions. Sixteen, seventeen years ago. I think that was also the time I first heard the band Bijelo Dugme, and the name became associated in my mind with Bjelo Polje in Montenegro, hometown of Gruban Malić, the central character of *Hero on a Donkey* and *War was Better*. It may also have been then that stores began carrying Montenegrin wine, which was red and either semi-dry or semi-sweet. And Bulatović was, after all, Montenegrin.

That combination of Balkan rock music, Balkan wine, and Balkan prose was so extraordinary that for me, Yugoslavia itself acquired the character of a semi-fantastical realm. In addition, people who'd been there said that the rocky limestone mountains (yes indeed, it was right there where they filmed all those Karl May adaptations) drop straight into a warm sea. For an inhabitant of the cold and windy central European plain, this was incomprehensible, especially considering both places were ruled by communists. After all, communism—at least the way I saw things—belonged in drab, temperate zones. For some time Yugoslavia captivated my imagination almost as powerfully as America. But America was too far away, too unreal, and had been thoroughly exploited from the point of view of the imagination. What can be thought about New York or California, when those places have been touched by every conceivable idea? Can you imagine yourself somewhere that everyone has already traveled to in their dreams? Hardly anyone, on the other hand—I reasoned—had traveled to Yugoslavia. At least in their dreams.

Yet all that passed.

> *"Did you feel me starting on you?" whispered Petar, half-conscious.*
>
> *"Just relax and eat," Jovan said with difficulty.*
>
> *"I've already finished the head," continued Petar in his fever. "Now it's time for the neck and the ribs."*
>
> *"Do I taste really bad?" asked Jovan, stumbling.*
>
> *"Now I'm getting close to the heart," groaned Petar. "You'll see what'll be left of you. Hold still and stop tripping up . . . That's it, like that."*

> *Jovan was weeping more and more*
> *hopelessly.*
>
> *They limped along, arms round each other's*
> *waists. They could barely keep on their feet.*
> *They struggled through a palpably dense song*
> *and through dandelion clocks with greater*
> *difficulty than through bushes and clouds.*
>
> *And the road before them was uneven and*
> *white.*

That's the end of *The Red Cock Flies to Heaven*. Petar and Jovan leave to go back where they came from, which is to say nowhere. These Slavic, Balkan incarnations of Vladimir and Estragon undertake their journey the way their Beckettian cousins undertook their waiting. Central Europe, Southern Europe, Eastern Europe—the worse Europe, in any case—was never able to come to a stop, to experience total immobility. It was always too young for this and could never understand that the world can be used up and come to a halt, just like that. The Montenegrin hoboes are the same at the end as they were in the beginning. They've passed through the heart of the tragedy and haven't changed one iota, because their lot is fate itself, not decline or redemption. Their sweltering white road probably runs all the way around the world, and wherever they find themselves, they'll never leave it. To convince yourself of this it's enough to pick up *People with Four Fingers*. This story is dominated by obsessive movement. The heroes chase around from one end of Germany to the other. They change trains and vehicles between Hamburg and Munich, between Cologne and Hanover they steal and then abandon automobiles, hire taxicabs, and hitchhike in a nightmarish *On the Road* of emigration across a no-man's-land that they hate and that they lay waste to because they're unable to return to their own homelands to create the same chaos there. And this unrequited love of accursed sons absolves them in their lowest moments.

> *"We're innocent," Kuznetsov began quietly, as Marković took off his boots and rubbed cortisone ointment on his feet. "Someone else is guilty of the murders we've committed. Everything we've done up till now and that we're still going to do is evidence of the guilt of others. We're powerless, no one is offering us their support. That's why we kill. How can I explain to you all that we'll continue to spill blood until you understand that our life in emigration is a punishment, and our transgressions are an accusation against you? Who is going to atone for our sins, and how?"*

An ecstatic and—however foolish this may sound—patriotic eros elevates their wretched existence to the level of saintliness. When in one demented murder scene the chieftain of chieftains Sándor Kolár perishes, his body is cut open and found to contain nothing but a large Hungarian heart that longs for Subotica in Vojvodina; while in his skull, in place of a brain, his killers find a Yugoslav passport ten years out of date, with a gold coat of arms on the cover. The entire novel is a kind of diabolic parody of St. Augustine's "love and do what you will," which here might be rendered as: one can do anything out of love for one's homeland; or better still: if there is no homeland, everything is permissible.

Bulatović's Balkan, or rather Central, or perhaps Eastern European novel is about homelessness. The homeland, the myth of the homeland, becomes a fundamental value for those who have nothing else. The nineteenth-century nation-state that was supposed to be the guarantor of all social, economic, cultural, intellectual, and political values becomes instead a substitute for them. In a world where power, like wealth, falls to the few, where no merit guarantees a reward, and justice becomes a commodity like anything else, the human heart—like the heart of Sándor Kolár—needs fortification. It needs something permanent, something available to everyone irrespective of their merits, of the political climate, of prestige, authority, or affluence. It may be that for the disinherited, this final grace is their place of birth. A law that says we are all born equal is as beautiful as it is impossible to enact. But the fact that we are all born in a particular place is hard to question. For many of us, if not the majority, this is the only incontrovertible foundation of our fate.

I probably would not have written this text if it hadn't been for the newspapers. During the first, and second, and third wars in the former Yugoslavia, from time to time you could read about the doings of one Željko Ražnatović, known as Arkan. His sorry life and even sorrier death was like something out of Bulatović's prose. Here was a common hoodlum, wanted in the West for robbery and assault, returning to the bosom of his homeland to fulfill his patriotic duty. The homeland was in need, and so it embraced him and rewarded him. His paramilitary force was named the Tigers, though they should have been called the Hyenas. I've seen several photographs of Arkan. In one of them he's posing with a tiger cub, in another he appears in a historic Chetnik uniform with sword and tall riding boots, and in yet another he's in the company of a nightclub singer and in his dark polo-neck sweater he looks like a black marketeer. In all three pictures his gaze is perfectly unthinking. Showmanship, kitsch, and barbarity were embodied in his person as in a living allegory. In his own way he may even have been a tragic figure, but one utterly devoid of any awareness of tragedy: in other words, one that was merely pathetic and foolish. His love of photographic poses and Serbian disco culture indicated a desire to be something more than he was. The archaic Chetnik uniform and the tiger cub in his arms make you think of vacationers having their picture taken by a cardboard palm tree in a third-rate resort. If it weren't for the real blood being spilled, we'd merely be watching a sad farce. He got several rounds in the head as he was leaving a

Belgrade bar. He wasn't even given a few minutes to grasp why he was dying and what for. Perhaps that was a mercy.

Oh, this Central European solitude! This perpetual orphanhood for which there is no cure, because medicine doesn't work retroactively and cannot bring back what has died. A perpetual, unrelenting solitude and abandonment. Post-Great Moravian solitude, post-Jagiellonian solitude, post-Austro-Hungarian solitude, post-Yugoslavian solitude, post-communist solitude. The loop of history round the button of the present. What kind of story can be patched together in a language whose grammar has no future tense? What comes out is always some kind of elegy, some kind of legend, a sort of circular narrative that has to return to the past because not only the future but also the present fills it with trepidation. Here the past is never at fault, it's always an absolution. Old Kuznetsov may well have been right when he spoke of innocence. Guilt is borne only by those who believe that their deeds will in some way continue to exist in the future. Memory and the image of fate as an inevitability protect us from the cold touch of solitude. When all's said and done, it's only that which has passed that truly exists, and at least partially corroborates our uncertain Central European existence.

In 1989, a German journalist asked Danilo Kiš: "On the subject of Yugoslavian writers, what do you think about Bulatović?" Kiš responded: "Blackness! The End! Like they say in the movies: cut!" I liked this violent reaction in an author one would have thought so "unviolent." In a whole book of interviews—over two hundred pages long—Kiš only loses his composure at that one moment. It couldn't really have been otherwise, since everything separated these two writers: their politics, their experiences, their positions in Yugoslavian literature, their worldviews, their styles—just about everything, with the possible exception of Montenegro, because Kiš's mother, like Bulatović, was from there.

I always admired both of them. I admired both, but Bulatović was closer to me, with his lack of restraint; with his style, which in *Gullo Gullo* for instance turns into unbearable mannerism, uncontrolled sentences that try to include everything yet often contain only empty, narcissistic variations; with his exuberant imagination that ends up merely multiplying its own phantoms. Bulatović was closer to me because he was forever describing failure, but in such a way that it was as if he himself had experienced it; whereas Kiš attempted to take the decline and defeat of humanity and subject it to intelligent analysis. When Kiš bridles at the very mention of Bulatović's name, it sounds as if Western rationalism were snorting at what Eliade called "the paroxysmal chaos of the Slavic soul."

As befits a cultured person, I take neither one side nor the other. Yet Bulatović is closer to me, because the form he uses to represent the world is unsettlingly reminiscent of the world as it is. In other words, the world belongs more to Bulatović's books than Bulatović's books belong to the world—which of course is a clear sign of insanity. Nevertheless, madness in literature that closely precedes the madness of the world is unsettlingly reminiscent of good health.

Poetics and Slaughter

2005 saw the seventieth anniversary of the birth of Danilo Kiš. He died of lung cancer in 1989. I have several hundred photographs of him, and in the majority of them he has a cigarette in his hand. It's quite possible he smoked till the very end. Though I may be wrong, because the last picture with a cigarette is from 1986. Reading his books, I can smell tobacco smoke. He was one of the great writers of the Serbian language, or, in those days still, the Serbo-Croatian language. Some even say he was the greatest.

In any case, a short while ago a conference devoted to his memory was held in Belgrade. I went.

Belgrade is an extraordinary city. We drove in from the northeast on a broad multi-lane highway across a bridge over the Danube. The city loomed on the horizon; it was starting to appear to us, but in some perverse way it managed to postpone its own beginnings. Everything seemed in place, yet something was wrong. There are no billboards, said Krzysiek. He was sitting next to me in the car. He was right. There was nothing. We were entering a metropolis of two million people and on either side of the road there was grayness—grass, low-grade housing, sun-scorched bushes, and hardly any sign that we were coming into contemporary civilization. No billboards, no immense signs—there weren't even any stores, showrooms, bathroom worlds, carpet kingdoms, no hypermarkets, no Ikeas, no Tescos, nothing. Belgrade was beginning without any ostentation. The air smelled of exhaust fumes from old Zastavas, Ladas, Yugos.

Once we crossed the bridge and were in the city things didn't change much, except the traffic got worse and the buildings became taller. The same gray austerity prevailed, and the confusion intensified. On Kneza Miloša there was the skeleton of a multi-story building. You could see clearly where the bombs had passed through the floors one after another. Corroded reinforcing rods poked out of the shattered concrete. All around, everyday life was going on: cars were driving along, people were heading home from work. The street itself was quite elegant. It led toward the Parliament, and was lined by embassies. No one was doing anything about the ruin. Before the bombings the building had housed the general staff. Perhaps the Serbs had decided to leave it as a monument to Western barbarity. Right there in the embassy district, so the whole world should know.

The conference had been organized by the Center for Cultural Decontamination—a worthy non-governmental institution with a record of opposition to Milošević. In an empty hall a group of writers sat at a table, read texts about Danilo Kiš, and spoke of the significance his work held for them. The public sat on chairs in the hall. There were no more than twenty people. The whole event was watched over by the police. On the plain white walls there was an exhibition of photographs from Srebrenica. For example, long rows of identical coffins covered with green cloth. Or pits filled with a tangle of decomposing human bodies. That was why the police were guarding us. So nothing bad would happen either to us or to the exhibition. The famous "Srebrenica tape" had surfaced only a week or two before. Serbia was disquieted. Belgrade was once again unable to sleep. That was why a handful of writers and a handful of spectators was being protected by the police. Actually, in the evening, when the readings and roundtables were over and tables with food and wine were set up in the cool courtyard, the policemen mingled with the novelists, poets, and essayists, and everyone discreetly sipped a glass of wine or a beer together.

We read and spoke about Danilo Kiš amid photographs of hundreds of corpses and coffins. It was quite a natural setting in which to reflect on his writing. Undeserved death, people killed as victims of ideology, the perverseness of a history that feeds on human flesh—these were the themes he returned to obsessively. He devoted his books to them, and for them he invented a language of overwhelming power. It may be that, in dying of cancer in 1989, he was granted something in the nature of grace. He was spared what would come next. Had he lived he would have seen his own worst nightmares come true. Instead of his lungs failing him, he would probably have died from a failure of his heart, from a failure of his soul. But before that, as a full-blooded writer, he would have beautifully and pitilessly described that very death of his.

The last ten years of his life Kiš spent in Paris. His books were already well known both in Europe and in America. It can be said he was a world-famous writer. As he was leaving his homeland, it arranged a rather chilly farewell. His *A Tomb for Boris Davidovich*, published a year before his departure, was subjected to harsh criticism that had little to do with literary analysis: rather, it was based on politics and writerly envy. But when, a decade later, he was dying in Paris, he wanted to return to Yugoslavia. He—the child of a Hungarian Jewish father and a Montenegrin mother, a child who had lost his faith because he couldn't understand how God could permit the endless suffering of his mother as she took three years to die of cancer—he wanted an Orthodox funeral and a burial in the cemetery in Belgrade. His wish was granted.

Belgrade is a strange city. A meeting aimed at honoring the memory of one of the greatest writers in the Serbian language is safeguarded by the Serbian police. Its participants feel a little like adherents of a forbidden cult meeting in the catacombs.

Those sitting in the audience are mostly friends. On the walls are photographs of pits filled with human remains, but the presenters talk of the poetics, phonetics, and imagery of texts whose most important feature was precisely an account of the paranoia and depravity of a power that feeds on corpses and slaughter.

Map

Some time ago, in a used bookstore I bought a map: Neue Verkehrskarte von Österreich-Ungarn, Freytag und Berndt, Wien 1900. That is to say, a travel map of Austro-Hungary.

The map is a hundred years old and very fragile. I've unfolded it only very rarely. Not more than five times in the last four years. So when I finally do open it, I stare at it for hours on end. Of course, eventually I'll take it to a picture framer and ask him to back it with canvas, but for the moment I just meditate on its frailty.

The moment I saw it I immediately thought of "The Timetable of Bus, Shipping, Rail, and Air Lines." The map shows all the railroad stations and stops in the entire empire, and all are named. For example, in sandy-yellow Bosnia, which admittedly was occupied, but because of that was somewhat imperial, there's really only one rail line. It's marked in purplish red and runs from Bosanski Brod to the border with Dalmatia, ending in Metković. In Doboj two short branches lead to Jajce and Tuzla. With the aid of a magnifying glass the tiny faded place-names can be made out: Suchopolje, Gračanica, Petrovoselo, Miričina, Došnica, Poračić, Lukavac, Bistarac, Bukinje, Kohlengrube . . . That's how things look on a map from a hundred years ago.

The most interesting part, though, is that every least stop, every village of half a dozen cottages, every godforsaken backwater where the train stops—even only the slow train, even only once a week—all those places are marked and labeled, all are preserved and their names can be read with a magnifying glass, just as if you were reading the past itself, or discovering the origins of a legend.

Did you know that in those distant times the stretch between Dobrljin and Banja Luka bore the title *Militärbahn k.u.k.*, that is to say, "The Imperial and Royal Military Railroad"? And there was nothing of the kind anywhere else in the empire.

Whereas in the vicinity of Sighetu Marmației, on the present-day border between Ukraine and Romania, amid the wooded Carpathian valleys, there was a twisting ten-stop line called *Mármaroser Salzbahn*, or "The Máramaros Salt Railroad." That sounds rather fine, don't you think: Salt Railroad?

Yet it takes a crumbling map to find such a wonder on the border between the former Galicia and the Kingdom of Hungary. Incidentally, Galicia is the same sandy yellow color as Bosnia.

"The Timetable of Bus, Shipping, Rail, and Air Lines" was an attempt to model the world on a scale of 1:1, an attempt to create it anew. My map, on the other hand, like any old map, incidentally, preserves the world and at the same time shows its disintegration, its passing. As I study it I'm gazing into a nothingness that my imagination wants at all costs to fill. This frail, moldering sheet of paper is reminiscent of human memory—weak, imperfect, prey to forgetfulness and dementia.

In a few days I'm going to pack my things, get in the car, and head for Belgrade. I'll drive through Slovakia, Hungary, and Romania. On the way I'll be thinking about my Austro-Hungarian map; I'll imagine it to myself and regret that it's so flimsy any journey could prove fatal for it. At the same time, I'll recall all the journeys I've made along the same route in the past—and superimposed on all this will be memories of readings about these parts, recollections of living and dead authors, literary landscapes and occurrences that—on a par with real ones, seen from the window of a train or a car—have created a most permanent and unrepeatable reality. And of course I'll take present-day maps, those road maps that age so extraordinarily quickly, maps that for all intents and purposes are disposable. Over the last ten years I've gone through umpteen maps of Slovakia, Hungary, and Romania. They just keep falling apart from being constantly folded and unfolded. They were swept away by the wind on the Great Hungarian Plain and soaked by rain in the Carpathians. Could there be a better metaphor for traveling than a worn-out map? Is there a nobler sort of journey than the kind that follows in the steps of an author whose books you admire? Yes, it's a pilgrimage. After all, pilgrimages are nothing more than the older sisters of regular journeys.

To travel is to live. Or in any case to live doubly, triply, multiple times.

Romania

In the Tisa Hotel in Sighetu Marmației, at one in the morning, the sleepy receptionist takes twenty-five euros and hands over a room key and a TV remote. The hotel is a beautiful neoclassical building that remembers the days of the Austro-Hungarian Empire. The lobby and the restaurant still boast stucco moldings and gilded plafonds on high ceilings. Yet the rooms are home to melancholy and decay. The walls are bare and dirty. Feeble electric bulbs provide a dingy light. There's no water in the bathroom. It will come only in the morning, and then it'll turn out that the toilet doesn't flush and the shower soaks the entire bathroom, including the lamp, which starts to give off sparks. You asked for a quiet room, not one overlooking the street, and the windows do in fact look out onto an overgrown yard. Except that there's a building site in the yard, and from six in the morning onward the scaffolding is swarming with workmen, while a backhoe is loading rubble into a dump truck. You begin the day by fixing the flush mechanism in the toilet and listening to the singsong shouts of the construction workers.

That's Romania: gilded plafonds and moldings and a broken toilet. Romania is a land of marvels. I've been there maybe a dozen times and I still haven't had enough. Romania is a fairy tale. Past, present, and future coexist there, and decay walks arm in arm with growth. The new is very much on the way, but the old survives equally well.

The same day that I repaired the toilet flush I drove to the town of Baia Mare and took a seat on its beautiful market square, where baroque and Secession stand unconstrainedly side by side. It was all being renovated and restored, so as to give the buildings back their Habsburg luster. In addition, Baia Mare is an important center for the mining and chemical industries. And right in the middle of this city of a hundred and fifty thousand people, amid the Secession and baroque and rococo architecture, I saw a man with a scythe over his shoulder. He was walking slowly across a broad deserted market square. He was followed by his long late-afternoon shadow. Over his other shoulder he carried a bag with his belongings. Despite the heat he wore rubber boots. It was harvest time throughout Transylvania and he was probably wandering the region in search of work. His presence in this urban setting was something utterly natural. No one paid any attention to him. He had walked out of olden times, in a moment he would enter the present, then soon afterwards he'd disappear again into the past. Yet in Romania past and present have different meanings than we might imagine.

"The Romanians are descendants of two great ancient peoples: the Geto-Dacians and the Romans." (Mircea Eliade)

"I believed, and I was perhaps not mistaken, that we had sprung from the lees of the Barbarians, from the scum of the great Invasions, from those hordes which, unable to pursue their march West, collapsed along the Carpathians and the Danube, somnolently squatting there, a mass of deserters on the Empire's confines, daubed with a touch of Latinity." (Emil Cioran)

Both these views are probably correct. The more frequently I travel there, the more firmly I believe it. Once, in the ancient ruins of Sarmizegetusa, where the legendary proto-Romanian Decebal repulsed the attacking Romans, I saw sheep grazing. Next to this temple of national memory there was a little wooden shithouse whose contents seemed not to have been emptied since the days of the Emperor Trajan.

That, precisely, is Romania. A land from the *Thousand and One Nights*. Nothing is self-evident here, and anything can turn out to be something else. This country, so proud of its past, continues to pretend. One time I was in the Danube delta. It's the absolute end of the earth, where nature rules all. In the summer the place resembles a kind of European Africa, a tropical swamp where everything is made of mud and reeds, everything is archaic, primal, pelicans fly across the sky and hundred-year-old catfish big as sharks lurk in the ooze. There are no roads. You get everywhere by boat. So one summer a twist of fate dumped me at a hotel built in the middle of the marshes. The boat pulled up to the bank and in the heart of that primeval land there appeared a greeter in miniskirt and high heels. Her heels sank into the mud, but she was resolutely coming down to meet the guests. She bore a tray with a welcoming drink. The exquisite little glasses contained *cujka*, a simple peasant slivovitz that's made in half the cottages in the country. But in each glass there was a green olive.

That is Romania. A country that seems taken aback by its own existence. On the highways there are the latest model Mercedes and Range Rovers, while on the roadsides old women walk along carrying baskets on straps like backpacks, and over their shoulders are wooden rakes and pitchforks whose shapes haven't changed in hundreds of years. Both the Range Rovers and the wooden pitchforks are completely real, because Romanian time is so ingeniously constructed that the notion of anachronism has no application here. Everything happens at the same time. In the shadow of the nuclear power station at Cernovodă on the Danube you can hear the rumble of carts drawn by donkeys, while herds of cattle wander across main roads. In the cities you can see country girls in folk costume, and in the villages boys dressed like rappers on MTV; from hopeless slums there emerge Gypsies with the pride and outward appearance of Spanish hidalgos: black hats, silver-studded belts, and cowboy boots with gold buckles . . . Yes, I like going to Romania because it's chaotic, elemental, unpredictable, paradoxical. Romania is a refreshing mental exercise for a mind grown used to banal and unimaginative solutions.

[Author's Note: The quotation from Eliade is the opening line from his book *The Romanians: A Concise History*. The Cioran quote is from his essay "A Little Theory of Destiny," collected in *The Temptation to Exist*.]

Montenegro

Budva lies on the Adriatic coast of Montenegro. I was there at the beginning of August. Budva is a resort. Its visitors are mostly Serbs. Montenegro is moving slowly towards independence. It wants to break away from Serbia, from Serbia's burdensome company and its blighted fate. No one likes Serbia, and Montenegro knows this only too well. Only Russia still likes Serbia a little. In just the same way as Montenegro likes Russia, as it happens. Though it's a purely platonic feeling, since Russia is far away and doesn't care a fig about some little Montenegro, which you can barely find on the map. For this reason, Montenegro has to set aside matters of the heart, and instead of the Russian ruble it has adopted the euro.

Yes indeed, the Balkans are a land of wonders: in a country that doesn't actually exist yet, in a country that only a few years ago was still engaged in a war, and on the wrong side to boot, in a country that was bombed by NATO planes, in a country whose chief source of income till very recently was smuggling, in a country about which Europe has only the foggiest notion, or none at all—in this country you pay for things in euros.

Everywhere. At the market, in stores, in taxicabs, and in hotels. It's in euros that wages are issued and in euros that bribes are paid. With euros you can rent a car or buy a donkey. In the resort of Budva, homemade suntan lotion is also paid for in the pan-European currency.

So anyway, in the summertime half of Serbia descends on Budva. There's also a handful of Albanians, a few Russians, and the occasional Pole, but the Serbs are the most important. Every day three or four Boeing 737s arrive from Belgrade. One of them is chartered from the national airline of Papua New Guinea. The Serbs are in a hurry. They want to make sure they get their dip in the Adriatic before their country becomes a landlocked island surrounded on all sides by countries and peoples who hold a grudge against Serbia, and vice versa. Perhaps this is why a summer vacation in Budva resembles an infernal carnival. Especially in the evenings, when the boardwalk along the seafront begins to pulse with lifeless mechanical music. Dozens of stands offer grilled sausage, *pleskavic*, and *ćevapčići*. Wood smoke rises into the air. This is a festival staged by a poor nation that until recently only ate meat a few times a year; it's a celebration of plenty, a vacation-time jamboree. BMWs and Mercedes containing guys in dark glasses edge into the human crowd—the larger and newer the model, the further they drive into the throng and the more ruthlessly they push the walkers aside. The drivers look like characters from a poor-quality contemporary commedia dell'arte: some of them model themselves on mafia godfathers, others on playboys, but both end up looking like pimps. In any case, they resemble caricatures of Italian characters from the pop culture imaginarium. They could always get Italian television here, and in Tito's time, all across Yugoslavia it seems, Montenegrins were considered the best-dressed citizens of the socialist republic.

Among the booths with roast meat and the cars that cost tens of thousands of euros, amid the funfairs with their merry-go-rounds and big wheels and roller coasters, amid the cadaverous electronic music and the half-naked women tottering on six-inch heels, children are sleeping. They lie on the sidewalk under blankets, and next to each one is a cardboard box for money. People pass by the tiny recumbent figures, step over them, occasionally toss ten or twenty cents into a box, and continue on their way. All around is the thudding of the mindless, catatonic music, but the kids do not wake up. They're most likely pumped full of drugs.

Close by, in an enclosure made of wooden pickets, where the light is brighter and the music louder, there's a discotheque. The place is so crowded that those trying to enjoy themselves can only stand in place, raise their arms, and wave them in time to the computerized din. Three yards away there's a woman with a ten-foot python round her neck and a man with a small monkey on his shoulder—you can have your picture taken with one creature or the other. The whole place—the beach, the boardwalk, and the resort—everything is immersed in a solution of restless stroboscopic light and electronic pandemonium. This is how Budva imagines modernity and the big wide world.

The hills begin just outside Budva. The road switchbacks up higher and higher. In a few minutes the resort and the disco and the six-inch heels have vanished and it's as if they never existed. From a tawdry imitation of the modern we shift into a completely real past. Donkeys graze by the road, while on sun-scorched hillsides goats look for something edible. In the desolate terrain there are stone houses with thick walls and windows like arrow slits. There's nothing strange about this: here the tradition of vendettas is still alive. Just like in Albania, which lies eighteen miles distant. At such times a house becomes a fortress and a last refuge. In this archaic landscape only the cars moving along the highway remind us that it is the twenty-first century.

This modernizing experiment seems to have something diabolic about it. Everything that was, becomes rejected in the name of a modernity that assumes the nature of a fiction, an illusion, a devilish apparition. To a greater or lesser extent this applies to all the postcommunist countries. But it's only in Montenegro that it can all be observed within the space of ten miles.

Pogradec

In Thanës we crossed the border on foot. On the Albanian side two old Mercedes were parked on a concrete-surfaced square. The ride to Pogradec was supposed to cost fifteen euros, but we bargained it down to twelve. The route followed the shoreline of Lake Ohrid. Across the water was Macedonia. It was hot. A solitary passenger car stood at a derelict railroad stop. The car had no windowpanes and it was ruddy with rust. The cab driver was silent. A woman was singing on the radio. As we drove into the town I suddenly realized that what she was singing was a Portuguese fado song. There are some coincidences that have the look of an exquisite plan.

The melancholy of the music and the melancholy of the town intermingled, and the image became permanently imprinted in my memory: low gray buildings, the chaotic bustle of the street, a cloudless sky, pale blue mist over the waters of the lake, and the low voice of the singer imbued with mournfulness. At the time I thought to myself that Portugal is in a sense similar to Albania. Both lie at the edge of a landmass, at the edge of a continent, at the end of the world. Both countries lead somewhat unreal lives beyond the main flow of history and events. Portugal can at best dream of past glory, and like Albania can long for a fulfillment to be brought by some undefined future.

A few pigs were trotting along the sidewalk. They crossed the roadway and scuttled off among the two-story apartment blocks. Further away, behind the flat roofs of the concrete neighborhood, rose the dome of a mosque. The town smelled of dust. It was late afternoon. We drove to the Tea Hotel, though this was an Albanian name and had nothing to do with the beverage. The far end of the street melted away in a pale blue glare. The air mixed with the waters of the lake and turned into a mist that, along with cement dust and a marshy smell, filled the alleyways of the town.

We had come here from Pristina in Kosovo. We'd been traveling all day, with transfers in Skopje and Struga. It was an expedition into the heart of unknown and unwanted lands. After all, who even goes to Kosovo? Who, aside from its inhabitants, and international bureaucrats and soldiers from every corner of the world? Who needs Kosovo? Or Macedonia? Small, forgotten countries that for some represent nothing more than a problem, and for others, plunder. When the world turns its gaze away for a moment they'll simply cease to exist, because today the only things that exist are those per-

ceived by others. Existence for its own sake has long stopped
having any meaning.

So then, Pogradec was the end of the world. A few miles
further on, Macedonia began. A little further still was Greece.
The town lay on a narrow strip of shoreline squeezed between
lake and mountains. In the late afternoon it looked beautiful
and sleepy. Elderly men, dressed with an elegance not of today,
were strolling along the lakefront promenade. They were all
wearing hats; their dark pants had a neat crease, and most of
them were in jackets despite the heat. They looked like a crowd
of extras from some French or Italian movie from the late fifties or early sixties. They were short and slim, with stern slender faces. They walked along in pairs or sat down to games of
chess in the shade of the trees. Each game attracted spectators
of the same age and in the same outfits.

In communist times, Pogradec was surrounded by gigantic mines of lead, nickel, and iron ore. In the 1960s, Chinese
specialists modernized the local mining industry. These men
must have remembered them. In their simple and somewhat
military spruceness they resembled retired engineers.

Enver Hoxha was paranoid; he took his tiny archaic country, on the periphery of European civilization, and closed it off
to the world, only to strike up an alliance with a global giant
that lay thousands of miles to the east, at the very limit of the
earth. The Albanians—who had lived for generations in their
hills and their tribal structures—for centuries had had no need

46

to look upon strangers, and here all of a sudden they had to stare into the face of a Maoist technocrat from China.

I wandered down the promenade and in the restrained gestures of the Albanian retirees I discerned traces of Chinese reserve. In the gardens there were stone pines, palm trees, rhododendrons, and villas in the Italian style. They were moderately dilapidated, in a state of partial collapse, and for this reason devoid of the typical ostentation of Mediterranean resorts. They were a memento of the times of Italian domination, from the beginning of the previous century. During the Second World War this domination turned into a full-blooded occupation and Pogradec became Perparimi, which means "progress." As far as toponomastic inventiveness is concerned, fascism was little different from communism. Apparently the Italians created the beginnings of the mining industry here, which was later perfected by the Chinese.

The women were relaxing separately. They sat on benches in the shade, their hands folded in their laps. Most of them had tightly fastened gray hair and dark dresses. In Poland, Slovakia, or Hungary, women like that can be seen in country churches. Here they were an element of the town landscape, but give them a rosary and they'd have looked like my grandmother getting ready for Sunday mass in the village of Gródek in Podlasie in eastern Poland.

Pogradec looked like a picture. As I walked along the promenade I felt as if I'd entered the work of a painter. Or a playwright. In the clothes, the faces, and the background there was a subtle displacement that turned the world, reality, Pogradec itself, into illusion. The landscape became outdoor scenery, the outfits costumes, and the faces and gestures masks and acting. Or to put it another way: Pogradec recalled a dream. Its reality was a little dulled at the edges, a little rounded. Pogradec also reminded you of a fairy tale, a story in which a miracle takes place, yet no one is surprised by it.

In the evening I went for a walk. The town had come alive. I counted pool halls. They were everywhere. On the first floors of apartment buildings, in empty concrete-built rooms, upstairs, on the second floor, the third. The click of balls came from brightly lit windows. Pogradec has about twenty thousand inhabitants. In the downtown area alone I counted about thirty pool joints, each with three or four tables. In some of them there were regular tables too and men sat at them playing cards, chess, and dominoes. Just like that. They came there to spend time, which they had more than enough of since the closing of the mines. Pool had taken over the town. That noble game, combining geometrical abstraction with kinetics, allows a person to forget the everyday. The men circled the tables like they were hypnotized. They moved back, moved forward, judged distances, stepped on tiptoe and held their breath as if afraid that the moving spheres would change direction and the cosmic harmony of the game would be disturbed.

A Shortage of Rain in the Accursed Mountains

It began when my Albanian publisher wrote: "Sorry, but your book won't be coming out when we planned; it'll probably be a month or two later. The thing is, in Tirana there are power outages for eight or ten hours a day."

I wrote back: "No worries, Sokol. And I have to say that's a pretty good reason for a delay. Other publishers' excuses aren't usually so convincing."

Then other Albanian friends reported that in the south, in Gjirokastër, there was no electricity for twelve hours daily, while in Kukës, up in the north, near the frontier with Kosovo, it was dark and cold for up to eighteen hours out of twenty-four.

Albania gets most of its energy from hydroelectric power plants—about 90% on a national scale. The biggest ones are in the north, on the Drin River. In Koman and Fierzë, huge dams and plants have been built, and the river's been transformed into a sort of narrow lake, a Balkan fjord. With a little good will and good luck, the entire width of northern Albania—from

Shkodër near the Adriatic to Kukës on the Kosovo border—is traversable by water. In a straight line it's only about sixty miles, but the dammed river twists and meanders, squeezing between mountain ranges, and as a result the journey takes all day. I've made it several times.

It's a beauteous and ancient piece of Europe. There are no roads. People get off the ship, a river ferry made out of an old boat and the bodywork of a bus, and pack mules are waiting for them on the shore. They load them up with everything that can't be produced locally. Plastic hoses, buckets, lamp oil, salt for preserving meat, and matches. Sometimes the loads are in wholesale amounts, and the animals stagger under the burden of Fanta bottles and cans of beer. Rocky paths rise up all the way to the sky, cross the passes, and disappear in the void of the mountains known as the Bjeshkët, or "Accursed." This summer, somewhere before Fierzë, I saw several dozen wedding guests—men in suits, women in high heels with fancy hairdos straight from the hairdresser—all in single file ascending a vertiginous path that zigzagged upwards to some lofty crest.

Sometimes, in the distance, isolated houses can be seen. They resemble four-sided stone towers capable of resisting a lengthy siege. The windows are thin as arrow slits. This isn't surprising, given that—till recently—you didn't ask about the number of people occupying a given house, but about the "number of guns" there . . . in other words, the number of men capable of bearing arms who lived under the same roof in a single multi-generational family. Homesteads are several hours' march from one another and are self-sufficient: they have their own flocks of sheep, their donkeys, their patches of corn, plum orchards so they can distill alcohol, small fields of tobacco, stocks of firewood, and hay for the animals. In essence, these places are a little like settlements of landlocked Robinson Crusoes. The solitude of the inhabitants is only multiplied by their numbers. Sometimes, on a deserted shore, you can catch a glimpse of a lone figure. The person waves and the ferry changes course, docks, and a long plank is laid down from the deck. The person comes on board and the passengers ask when he left home. "Before dawn," replies the new arrival.

In this most archaic of regions, electricity is produced—energy for the whole country. Energy—the symbol of progress and modernity—is born in a place where people live enclosed in social structures of families and clans, their existence regulated by medieval laws of custom that are much stronger than official state statutes. It's from here that electric power flows to the cities, to Shkodër, Tirana, and Durrës, bringing to life the innards of factories, computers, televisions, and ATMs. Amid the rugged landscape stand immense pylons. They're black and rusted. Last year someone blew some of them up. My Albanian friends were unable to say who did it or why.

Now there's no water in the lakes, and the turbines stand idle.

The north never enjoyed a good reputation. Central and southern Albania saw it as a breeding ground of lawlessness, violence, savagery, and ignorance. Demons were said to dwell there. It wasn't a place to go to without a good reason. Rather, people came from there—semi-mythical mountain folk who reached unscrupulously for power, money, and influence in the more civilized parts of the country. And then they fled back north when things grew too hot for them.

And now civilized and modernizing Albania sits around in dark cafés and bars, in front of dead computers, in fancy unheated apartments, growing bored without its casinos, waiting for rain, which will fall in the north and fill the lakes to the brim. And it's just like once before, long ago, when people gazed at the sky anticipating either harvest or hunger.

And I too am waiting with my publisher for rain to fall in the Accursed Mountains.

Rudňany

This is a story from Slovakia.

You have to get to Spišská Nová Ves, then drive six miles further into the mountains. On the way you pass Markušovce, with its rococo palace that belonged to the Máriássy family of Hungarian magnates. Its fairytale outline amid the decaying buildings looks a little surreal. Outside the main palace building Gypsies pull carts loaded with firewood they've gathered. At the other end of the palace grounds is a small summer castle that one of the Máriássys built for Kaiser Joseph II at the end of the eighteenth century. The Kaiser was supposed to visit, and an appropriate setting was needed for his majestic presence. He never came. Today, from the windows of the restored castle you can look out over the road and the river, in which Gypsy women are washing colorful rugs while their dark-skinned children play in silvery splashes of water.

But it's still a ways to Rudňany. You drive into the depths of the valley and it gets darker and darker. On the right-hand side you pass ruined warehouses—large concrete blocks with dozens of broken windows. They look as if they've been dead and cold for a long time. Railroad tracks run alongside and you can see derelict cars and rusty loading platforms and gantries. Immediately after this lifeless industrial scene, green mountains rise up, and if a person set his mind to it he could follow paths and hiking trails through the woods and in a day or two he'd reach the Hungarian border to the south. This time, though, Rudňany has to suffice as a destination, and when the valley narrows even more you notice people living in this lunar landscape. Smoke rises from brick huts that were once outbuildings of the railroad station, blackening makeshift roofs assembled from scraps of corroded iron sheeting. Swarthy kids scuttle about amid smoldering heaps of refuse. It's hard to tell whether they're simply playing, or whether they're trying to dig something from the piles of trash. The earth here smokes, emitting a stench, and you have the impression that the children's skin has been blackened by the smoke. If it weren't for their rapid motions and their cheerfulness you might think you were entering into hell.

Yet, in fact, Rudňany is a mining village next to an inactive mine. Silver, mercury, copper, and iron were extracted here for seven hundred years. Now it's all dying. There is nothing beautiful here. The drab buildings of the town are still there on the right-hand side, crammed into the tapering valley. The road zigzags uphill. At its end you can see that over the course of those centuries people scooped out the inside of the mountain, removing rocks and ore and leaving an immense hole in the ground. The Gypsies live at the bottom of the hole. Their dwellings—a cross between shanties and wattle huts—lie in the depths as if they'd been thrown there at the whim of some malicious demiurge. Down there the day begins later and ends sooner. The rock walls rise vertically for a hundred feet. There's no doubt about it—this is what hell looks like. A hell that someone has populated and is trying to inhabit. A thousand Gypsies have built a settlement that is a miracle of improvisation. The shacks, huts, shanties look as if the wind might sweep them off at any moment, as if they could be washed away by the rain. People who possess nothing have taken residence in a pit from which everything of value has already been removed, leaving only barren earth. And so it is that those who have nothing live in a place where there is nothing.

The extreme poverty there was turning into something like a metaphor. I'd never seen such a blighted place where life was still being lived so normally. Alongside the road, a hundred feet above, on the surface of the earth as it were, there was a large concrete square and a handful of dingy ruined buildings that must have been what was left of the mine's offices. The square was filled with hundreds of people walking about, stopping, and chatting, as if on the Corso. They had no other occupation and so they were simply spending time with one another. It looked like an allegory of Sunday or of a holiday in general. The crowd was animated, dressed up, colorful, and at the same time listless. No one needed them and so they occupied themselves with each other. They killed time together.

I watched them and imagined the future of the world, with its growing numbers of people of whom it will be said that they're simply superfluous, because there's no work for them, there's no room, no prospects, and actually we're closing up shop just now and don't anticipate reopening. Those who arrive late will have to stand or stroll around and talk for whatever time is still remaining, or for eternity, on a concrete square.

Yet their numbers will be so great that the world may find itself divided into two parts, and one will have to be shut away from the other. I mean, does anyone need Africa, for instance? Surely only mercenaries, the Foreign Legion, and diamond traders. And dreamers who in their childhood fantasize about distant journeys. For the rest, Africa might just as well not exist. Just as the Gypsies of Rudňany might as well not exist, with their ahistorical presence, their lack of literacy or of a state of their own. Though as far as the latter is concerned, you never know: demographers claim that, given the Gypsies' natural population growth, in fifty years—not just in Rudňany, but in Slovakia as a whole—they'll end up constituting a majority. And in this way, Poland may end up sharing its southern border with the first Gypsy state in history.

The Carpathians

I've lived in the Carpathians for seventeen years, and I've learned to think of them as a separate country or even continent.

I walk out of my house in the morning, look at the fresh snow, and start to clear the driveway so I can drive my daughter to school, or go to the store, or simply get out and about. I wield the shovel, put snow chains on the car, turn on the four-wheel drive, and try to make it through the snowdrifts to the road below, which was cleared by a big tractor in the night. All around is emptiness and quiet. A few hundred yards away, a thin column of smoke rises vertically from my neighbor's chimney. This is the only movement in the vicinity.

So I clear the driveway and I think to myself that at this same moment snow is being shoveled by any number of Slovaks, Ukrainians, and Romanians who live in the heart of these extraordinary mountains, which on a map look like the backbone of Central Europe. And not just by them—it's also being shoveled by Germans and Hungarians in Romanian Transylvania, and by Gypsies, who live everywhere.

To live in the Carpathians is to live in solitude and at the same time to have a sense of remote community. Not far from my home are peaks called Magura, Dziamera, and Kornuta—these names have wandered here along the Carpathian crest all the way from the Balkans, perhaps from ancient Macedonia or long-ago Albania. They were brought to my area by nomadic shepherds in the days when there wasn't a living soul here. These names cannot be found anywhere outside the Carpathians, and though they recur in four or five languages, they've never left the mountains.

In the Carpathians, expanses of space are intertwined with distances in time. Slovak, Polish, Ukrainian, and Romanian shepherds have changed very little for centuries. In their shelters high in the mountains cheese is produced by the same archaic method and using the same simple tools. Out of all the inventions of modern civilization, they've only adopted battery-powered flashlights, battery-powered transistor radios, and rubber boots. Nothing else changes, because there's no reason for it to. More, over a tract of six hundred miles or so, the shelters and the shepherds themselves don't change either. In Poland, in Ukraine, and in Romania, their day, their work, their timetable barely differ. They even smell the same: of bonfire smoke, sheep manure, and cheese. I've smelled them in Poland and Ukraine and Romania, and I know what I'm talking about. I've driven six hundred miles and encountered a human smell identical to one I can find a mile from my home.

The Carpathians belong to four or even five countries, but at the same time they don't belong to anyone. They live their own archaic life. In our world there are fewer and fewer old things and places. Before long we'll lose the memory of where we came from and we'll never believe that, not so very long ago, our bodies emitted the same odor as the bodies of Romanian shepherds.

These are the thoughts that come to me as I shovel snow in the morning. It's winter, and I remember the village of Rășinari in Transylvania in the southern Carpathians. I went there two years ago in August because I wanted to see the birthplace of the wonderfully ironic and acerbic Romanian philosopher Emil Cioran.

Rășinari smelled of hot oil, fried onions, pig and horse manure, hay, and herbs. On hot afternoons this extraordinary combination made one's head spin. At dusk the animals would come down from their pastures. They would enter the village along the main road and find their farms. In the vanguard were huge, glistening black oxen. Behind them came several dozen speckled cows with swollen udders, and at the very end a small flock of frisky, playful goats. This daily parade was like a holiday. The whole village came out of its homes onto the road and watched the passage of the livestock. Children, old women in headscarves, men in small groups smoking cigarettes—everyone watched as the animals unerringly found their way to their own farms and stood by the gate waiting to be let in. This ritual had been repeated for centuries and everything in it was self-evident, complete, and in its own way perfect. Neither the animals nor the people made any superfluous movements.

After the herds had passed, the asphalt highway was coated with dung and urine. In the last rays of the sun it shimmered like glass. The infrequent cars had to be careful at the curves because it was slippery as ice.

That which was animal had entered into the heart of that which was human, and this was only proper, because in a natural everyday way, it recalled the memory of our beginnings.

I clear the snow and recall journeys I made long ago. The point is that from a Carpathian perspective even a six-hundred-mile journey is like a trip to the next village. Maybe there ought to be something like Carpathian nationality or Carpathian citizenship.

Though in fact, to live in the Carpathians is to remember that citizenship or nationality were always of little importance here. At times, in my extravagant cosmopolitan dreams, I see the main ridge of the mountains. I leave my home and head east, then south, and I don't encounter any borders. On the way there are only flocks of sheep, shelters, sheepdogs—and in the winter even those things aren't there. Across the ridge, along the deep valleys, there are several rail lines and several roads linking different countries. Both the roads and the tracks look like a prank, like extraterritorial corridors leading to the other side of the mountains. The noisy, restless flow of modernity passes through them, but the mountains themselves remain undisturbed.

Parody as a Continent's
Means for Survival

Why does the East of Europe want money from the West? Why is no one talking about anything else? Why are the newspapers I buy and the radio I listen to filled with percentages, figures, balances, and reports of meetings at which some people tried to obtain as much as possible while others strove to give as little as possible, after which both the first group and the second group proudly announce that they didn't yield an inch? Maybe there's something wrong with my radio, maybe I buy stupid newspapers, maybe where you live things are different. Maybe where you live you have conversations about the export of Gothic cathedrals, the transfer of spirituality, the shipping of the Mediterranean and Greco-Roman tradition, consignments of values and paradigms and founding myths worthy of the third millennium, whereas here we know nothing of any of that, and so our vision extends only to ATMs operating like perpetuum mobiles, and to hypermarkets in which, along with free goods, they also give you cash. But maybe we're just foolish and we missed something, maybe our barbaric minds failed to perceive all the finer points of this gigantic plan that's supposed to transform the continent.

Was it really the case that nothing else attracted us? Nothing aside from neat clothing, clean streets, income that exceeds expenditure, and an infinite number of ways of overcoming boredom when boredom finally becomes our lot? Have our desires become confined to the soteriology of equalizing Gross Domestic Products from Kiev to Lisbon? Was our unity really meant to be so hollow and devoid of content that the unrestricted flow of goods, services, and capital must fill it up entirely? All these things seem stillborn. Is anyone happy with such a state of affairs? We have to become you, but do you want to be us? That is questionable.

It may be that my part of the continent possesses an instinct that guards it against gradual destruction: you can see it disappear before it even comes into existence, no more than a reflection or caricature now of something larger and stronger than itself. After all, no one expected *you* to be the ones who would change; rather, it was us who would have to repeat your gestures, your victories, and your mistakes. It is indeed a magnificent path, but it deprives us of the right to our own accomplishments and failures, even if the former are mediocre and the latter ignominious.

This instinct of ours also lets us know that, in taking from you that which is most unsophisticated, we will not be exposed to ridicule, because we'll be doing exactly what is expected of us. In becoming a crooked mirror, we confirm the full majesty and uniqueness of the original.

It's true—old Europe is fixated on itself and its own virtues. But is it possible to be virtuous forever? Is it possible to improve, with impunity, that which already seems perfect, or to develop that which is already developed, without risking hypertrophy? For more than half a century, this image of old Europe has been lacking a blemish, a fault. It can safely be said that old Europe was so preoccupied with itself it didn't have time to commit a single sin. Horrified by its own past, it was intent on recovering its innocence at any cost. It probably succeeded. It avoided hatred like the plague, at the same time reducing other emotions to a necessary minimum. Extending the realm of freedom into infinity, it blundered into a contradiction by which it found itself restricted by its own lack of restrictions. It was precisely this that drove it to regions where the supply of freedoms will probably exceed the demand. To put it another way, there'll be so many freedoms that no one will be capable of consuming them in their entirety without risking death through overeating. Freedom has become a commodity whose availability, paradoxically, keeps society in check. The threat of its loss seems to enable us to tolerate its imposition.

We here have little faith in ourselves or in the future. Time always came to us from outside and was fashioned of a homogeneous substance, so we never had any reason to believe it would be different at the end than at the beginning. Nor did we hold common sense in excessive regard. It was common sense, after all, that suggested to us our situation was hardly to be envied. That was why we placed greater importance on emotions, which change one's image of the world without changing the world itself. The risks involved in change simply seemed too great and too futile. The story of change in this part of the continent is, after all, the story of failure. True, we failed together, but afterwards we could only look on enviously as you rose from your knees. It's easier to share a defeat (such a move produces a clear profit) than a victory.

Our faith in European unity and solidarity is moderate. In abandoning our own past we dismiss it as paltry and useless. Is it needed by anyone aside from ourselves? Would anyone else want to inherit it, just as we loudly and ostentatiously acknowledge your heritage? To put it plainly, was Paris for example moved by the experience of the failure, collapse, and disintegration of the European East as powerfully as the same East felt the very existence of that exemplary Paris? Did London, for instance, allow itself to think that the hell of the Balkans was not an exotic tribal affair but a tragedy just as European as that of Coventry in 1940 and 1941?

These questions may sound like complaints, but they're not. They speak only of the West's provincialism, which leads it to perceive the rest of the continent as a failed copy of itself. In the meantime the East takes from you only what it needs. It takes appearance, mask, and costume, with which it will be able to imitate you. Nothing more was ever expected of us, and the task was rather straightforward. We were perceived as an undifferentiated mass divided by obscure and unstable borders, and we didn't have to exert ourselves particularly in accepting the challenge. No one could tell our faces apart anyway, and so pretending to be someone else came easily to us.

If the West was parochial, then we practiced something that might be called pathological cosmopolitanism. We lived in our cities and countries in appearance only, because for us they were fictitious entities. They did not exist in and of themselves. Real life happened elsewhere, in the West. Our world was unreal. We had to make it so, because otherwise we would have had to despise it. Attempts to render our world more real resulted in sorry expeditions into an idealized past, or a hazy millenarianism that proclaimed the imminent arrival of a miraculous hybrid—the three-headed dragon of social equality, universal prosperity, and absolute freedom.

So then, in the realm of time it was always the future or the past, while in that of space, it was always "elsewhere." We were and still are cosmopolitans. If we want to be somewhere, it's "in Europe," or maybe at home, but best of all is to live in an imagined heroic past. We hate "now" and "here," and we love "elsewhere" and "at another time," up to the moment at which the one and the other actually arrive and become a hated present. We've never been able to accept ourselves as we are.

Whenever I try to imagine the future of my part of the continent, I'm visited by images of gentle, painless destruction: everything that made up these regions is going to disappear.

There's to be no more disorder, untidiness, irresponsibility, insouciance; there's to be an end to the perverse love of a jinxed history; our proclivity for confabulation is to disappear; our fondness for invention is also on the way out; while our penchant for fictions will be replaced with trust in a once-and-for-all conferred reality. In a word, what will perish is the world that we have patiently constructed, a world whose existence was our greatest accomplishment and triumph, because it was unique and unrepeatable. From a "European" point of view this world may well look something like an anti-world. Nevertheless, we were the ones who created it, and masterfully pioneered the art of living among its scenery and props.

And so I see a balance sheet involving losses rather than gains. I see things that are to vanish and in my imagination I can't replace them with anything else. For instance, what can take the place of complete disinterestedness? The sitting around, the waiting out of days and hours in the conviction that reality continues independently of our accomplishments and our struggles? When it comes down to it, this is simply a noble belief in the existence of things greater and more important than ourselves.

Or what can replace daydreaming, the exceptional ability to impose our own imaginings on conclusions suggested by reason?

What can we use to replace that magnificent sense of superiority we feel with regard to everyone else in the world, especially our closest neighbors—something that allows a person to survive every possible failure?

What can replace our hatred of ourselves? What can replace that great feeling, which forces us to abandon our own fate and step beyond it?

I could extend this litany into infinity, enumerating attributes and aspects of life in our part of the world. And once I was done with ideas, I could list objects that are to disappear for good, leaving no progeny and with no reasonable successors or substitutes.

What, for example, can replace the immortal horse harness, something that till now has acted as our coat of arms, and which the West stamped on most of the reports it received from these parts?

And what about all the rest of the animality that's embedded so deeply in our lives? What about the cattle that live so close to humans? What about the herds of cows returning at dusk from their pastures, lifting their tails and shitting in the middle of the village? What about the cattle smell, which reminds us where we really came from? When that disappears, when it vanishes from our everyday existence, there'll be nothing left that is capable of assuaging our loneliness.

And what about decay? What about the fragile material of our homes, which crumbles before our eyes because it's trying to accompany us as we age and die? What about our cities, which look like they were being demolished and constructed at the same time? What about impermanence and what about time, which hereabouts enters into objects in order to destroy them from within, and all this so that in the hour of his death a person shouldn't feel so terribly forsaken, knowing that he can die in the company of his possessions?

I cannot picture all this being replaced one day with something else. And for some time, this takes my thoughts away from the gentle destruction of my part of the continent. It may be that everything I've mentioned is simply irreplaceable and so will have to remain.

After all, Europe cannot be composed exclusively of the present. Yet everything suggests that the obsession with the present is ravaging life in the West and is starting to do the same to our own lives. There's something unhealthy in those old European cities that have abided continuously for seven or eight hundred years: amid the hieratic buildings, in a space filled with a concentrated past, beneath the venerable gaze of the bygone, there's a crowd obsessed with nothing more than the present moment. People look like insects preoccupied only with survival. They have no past because they're unable to learn anything from it, nor any future, because the future is constantly turning into the present.

All right, let's set ideas aside.

I'm going to try and tell you about something real. A few hours ago I came back from Slovakia. I often drive there, because the border is only ten miles away. Last week was a troubled one in that country. In Trebišov and several other places, Gypsies looted stores and fought with the police. It was all because, as part of its reform program, the Slovak government reduced family benefits by over fifty percent. Not just for the Gypsies, for everyone. Slovakia has 5.4 million inhabitants. Half a million of these are Gypsies. The Gypsy population is growing at a much faster rate. It's predicted that in fifty years they'll constitute the majority in Slovakia. In this way, the idea of a Gypsy state will become a reality. Slovaks are afraid of this, and you can understand them. After all, theirs is a youngish nation. It was fashioned in the nineteenth century. They codified their language, and they said straight out: as a nation we are not Czechs and as a political organism we are no longer Upper Hungary or Czechoslovakia, even though for centuries we were the first, or the second, or the third. Now, in front of Slovak stores, and in front of the Slovak police, there's a crowd of dark-skinned men and women who came from India seven hundred years ago and who are now attempting to disturb the sacred right of property, and trying to destroy a political and social order that's only existed for ten or fifteen years. The Gypsies are simply trying to take what they believe is theirs: other people's property. In their view, if property doesn't belong to the Gypsies it doesn't belong to anyone. Such a conviction is one of the basic elements of their culture—which, furthermore, is considerably older than Slovak culture, and is exceptionally resistant to change and outside influence. After all, they've survived several hundred years in a maximally hostile environment virtually unaltered. They've survived the perils of extermination and the lure of assimilation. They've taken a few gadgets from us, a little bit of the trash of civilization, but they never really had any desire to participate in the "European cultural heritage." It seems this wasn't of any particular interest to them.

But I saw no traces of the Gypsy rebellion. Everywhere was calm. It was just that you could see police and army patrols in the villages and towns. In the sleepy landscape of eastern Slovakia, these pallid young lads in uniform looked a little out of place, as if they'd gotten lost and were themselves in need of help.

I drove to the town of Krompachy to see the extraordinary settlement on its steep rocky slope. It looked like a colony of birds nesting on a cliff. The Gypsies built it out of waste materials, scrap, stuff that people had thrown away because it was of no use to them anymore: rusty sheet metal, old planks, rotting wooden beams. By what miracle it all managed to stay in place instead of blowing away in the wind, I don't know. Yes indeed, it was a miracle, a Gypsy victory over the laws of gravity. On the other side of the road, in the broad flat valley of the Hornad River, the children from this lofty settlement were at play. There was a slight thaw, ideal weather for making snowmen and snow castles. I couldn't believe my eyes: on the broad white meadow there were dozens of huge white balls. The dark children were still rolling new ones. It looked as though they

were trying to clear all the snow from the meadow in this man-
ner. It was beautiful and unreal. The balls were about three
feet in diameter, and they were strewn across the empty white
space as if they'd fallen from the sky. A little further away rose
the buildings of an ironworks with a towering chimney. The
kids were playing in its shadow. The two images could not be
linked together by any means. The children had created their
own space, which lay outside of time, just as their parents and
their whole nation lived outside of time. The simplicity of that
exuberant game, the wonderful prodigality of energy, the dis-
interested exertion for the sake of creating dozens of unneces-
sary and short-lived objects—all this meant that the presence
of the gloomy industrial structures seemed an absurd illusion,
a sick person's dream.

An hour later I was in Levoča. Cops were wandering around
on the ancient market square amid the leafless trees. They'd
been sent to maintain order in the Gypsy neighborhood to
the south of the town. But nothing was happening. The square
was the same as always. The three dogs and five police officers in field uniforms were bored to death. The Alsatians, at
their masters' commands, jumped sleepily back and forth over
park benches, or retrieved snowballs. If it hadn't been for the
uniforms, the guns, and the high-laced boots, the whole thing
would have looked like a lazy after-dinner siesta enacted by
decent townsfolk and their four-legged friends.

I sat in the Three Apostles Café and stared out the window.
For an hour nothing changed. The soporific park scene con-

tinued unabated. The well-fed, armed police with their shaved heads were turning into schoolboys. They threw snowballs at trees and at each other. The dogs were given ever-sillier commands: they lay on their backs and played dead. It all looked innocent and at the same time sinister. It was ambiguity personified. Brute force, tedium, and play were combined in perfect proportions, but instinct told you that any one of these three elements could take over at any moment, and for no particular reason.

As I returned home at dusk I thought about the Gypsies. Truth be told, I think about them often. As I travel I look for their impermanent, hopeless settlements—in Slovakia, in Romania, in Hungary. Their presence disquiets me yet at the same time arouses my admiration. When I consider their marginal existence, the gravity of my "Europeanness" is radically challenged. Here is a dark-skinned, unlettered people that for centuries has been passing through Europe and Europeanness as though these were poor, sparsely populated, unattractive lands. From time to time they come upon something they can make use of, but mostly it looks as though they already have all they need with them. Everything suggests that they've learned nothing from us and that they're unimpressed by the things we're so proud of. Can it be that for over six hundred years they've remained blind and impervious to our accomplishments? Can it be that they have sought out and settled in barren regions whose only advantage is that they can be successively abandoned? It's unbelievable that our world should be so very uninteresting. It's inconceivable that there should have been no attempts at imitation, that there's been no effort, however unsuccessful, to copy us! To treat thousands of years of our civilization as no more than a campground and a source of profit!

If there'd been some barbarian menace in all this, some hatred of the savage for the civilized man, a desire for revenge or destruction . . . but no: it's merely indifference, merely a lack of interest.

I'm not at all trying to suggest that we here, in the East, are a little like Gypsies—though that's an intriguing comparison.

Nevertheless, it's hard for us to regard Europe as a whole as something that belongs to us, as our homeland, our inheritance. We are strangers in it; we come from outside, from lands about which Europe itself has only the vaguest notion and which it treats more like a threat than as a part of itself.

On our side, it's not much better. As we look at you we see our own future. In this way our life becomes dull, devoid of mystery and excitement. We were unable to accompany you in your flowering and your growth—instead, we will ape your decline.

If there's something fascinating in what's going to happen, it's our own mistakes that we are going to commit. Our continental mission may well be the deformation of your achievements, their disintegration—a grotesque transformation and a parody of them that will serve to extend their life.

A Zone of Mixed Populations

Albanians, Belarusians, Bosnians, Bulgarians, Croats, Czechs, Estonians, Hungarians, Latvians, Lithuanians, Macedonians, Moldavians, Montenegrins, Poles, Romanians, Serbs, Slovaks, Slovenes, and Ukrainians—this is more or less how you can describe the map of the territories inhabited by two hundred million new Europeans. To ensure the task isn't too easy, let's add to this "zone of mixed populations"—as Hannah Arendt called the mutable and amorphous expanses lost somewhere between Germany and Russia—the colonies of those very Germans and Russians scattered here and there; let's also add, say, the Gagauz and the Aromuns, let's add the restless and international Gypsies, the Tatars of the Crimea, and the Turks who failed to return to their unexpectedly diminished homeland on the Bosphorus in time.

Yes indeed, two hundred million new Europeans is a real challenge. It ought to drive the sleep from people's eyes and fill them with anxiety and joy, because what will happen next will resemble the discovery of an entirely new continent.

The plan for the first decades is more or less as follows: The Gypsies will arrive and set up their camps in the middle of the

Champs Elysées. Bulgarian bear-handlers will demonstrate their tricks on the Ku'damm in Berlin; half-savage Ukrainians will establish misogynistic Cossack communities on the Padan Plain at the gates of Milan; drunken prayer-addled Poles will lay waste to the vineyards along the Rhine and the Mosel and in their place will plant bushes bearing fruits filled with pure alcohol, then they'll move on, singing litanies, and will only come to a stop at the very edge of the continent, in the Catholic city of Santiago de Compostela, famed for its miracles. It's hard to say what'll be done by the Romanians, with their million-strong herds of sheep—their national attribute is sheep-herding, but even more than that, unpredictability. The Serbs, Croats, and Bosnians will cross the English Channel in their Dalmatian pirogs and Balkanize Britain, which will once and for all, as the Lord God intended, be divided into Scotland, England, and Wales. The inhabitants of Latvia and Lithuania will contrive to change their identities over and again, thereby misleading public opinion, which is accustomed to unambiguous labels. The Slovenes and Slovaks will present themselves as inhabitants of Slavonia, and in this fashion reduce all the computer systems of the European Union to despair. The Moldavians, whose main source of income is the sale of their own bodily organs, will convert their entire nation into capital and thereby bring ruin to the world transplant market. And what the Albanians will get up to is beyond human ken . . .

My friend Yuri Andrukhovych, the excellent Ukrainian novelist and poet, once said that when a writer from Central or Eastern Europe comes to the West he finds himself in a perfect situation, from a literary point of view: he can tell the most outrageous stories about his country and his part of the continent, he can spin the most fantastical tales, present them as God's honest truth, and then simply rest on his laurels, since his stories will never be subject to verification—partly because his audience suspects that in his part of the world anything at all really can happen, but also partly because, for this audience, the very existence of that region is highly problematic and already resembles a literary fiction.

The immediate future of Europe is indeed an encounter with fiction, with a fiction populated by two hundred million entirely real beings. In such a situation, discussions that take place in Paris, Berlin, or London about the future shape of Europe look rather anachronistic. Before long the continent will change beyond recognition and will never be the same again. I'm a long way from ascribing some special potential to the Moldavians, the Poles, or the Central European Gypsies. I'm just trying to think of this part of the world as a particular whole that—if only with the force of its own inertia—will manage to change the face of the continent. These unfamiliar and exotic tribes will soon find themselves within the space of Europe, but it would be naïve to imagine that they'll give up their customs, their defects, their impetuous desires, their grudges, their fantastical illusions, their unique temperaments—in a word, that they'll renounce their individual characteristics in favor of certain liberal and democratic European universalities. Their situation recalls that of the barbarian conquerors before whom the gates of the city were opened because this was the only wise thing to do. Do you remember Constantine Cavafy's poem "Waiting for the Barbarians"?

And so things are shaping up for a long and beautiful decline. It'll be a while before the new tribes appearing out of nowhere will have had their fill of the spoils, before they process them and adapt them to their own needs, improving them and eventually turning them into a parody of themselves. But before this happens, old Europe will experience a second youth. As it loses popularity in the world, for a while it will regain it in its own eyes. Affluence, security, order, satisfaction, and refinement will be exported the way cars, clothing, and food have been traded thus far. It goes without saying that these complex, fragile, immaterial commodities will continue to require modifications to suit the unpredictable tastes of such distant and unknown peoples; efforts will need to be made to keep them attractive. At least until the farthest reaches of the continent have mastered the art of independent local production.

It's possible that at that stage, old Europe will cease to be needed. For want of anything better to do it'll occupy itself with its own history, remembering its former importance and greatness. In a paradoxical way it will repeat the lot of its younger sister, who till recently was wrapped up completely in her own past—which by contrast constituted a series of failures, disappointments, and injustices of fate. It will also repeat its sister's lot in that it will experience a sense of being superfluous. Debtors rarely show gratitude. The moment they stand on their own two feet they assign all the credit to themselves, and their memory miraculously erases their past moments of abasement.

Is it possible to merge two streams of history that have flowed separately alongside one another for so long? It frequently happened too that when one ran faster, the other virtually stopped moving, drying up or becoming an underground watercourse. Nations do not remember general history and feed only off their own. The same is true of the future. We can plan it together as a shared enterprise, but when it arrives it immediately turns into the past, and at that moment it becomes nothing more than our own personal property. Because we don't have anything else.

Stróże

I sometimes drive to Stróże to pick someone up or drop them off at the station. The departures board lists Košice, Budapest, and in the right season, even Bucharest. The front of the station building is watched over by a noisy little mutt. Inside, especially in winter, there's a massive homeless man. A woman cuts color photographs out of old illustrated magazines. Stróże is a railroad junction. One line runs south; not far from Leluchów it crosses the Poprad River and the Slovak border. The other line leads east, passing through Gorlice, Jasło, Sanok, Ustrzyki, and Krościenko on its way to Ukraine. In the station cafeteria, at one time there used to be a pinball machine. Boys from the country and boys on their way home from school would stand round it in a tight circle. Inside the machine, colored lights would be flashing. It was like seeing a great metropolis in the night. The boys wore thin black leather jackets. Railroad workers in overalls would come in to have some soup, *bigos*, or hot kielbasa. They'd talk with each other about their work, their neighbors, their wives. Freight cars from Romania, Hungary, and Slovakia wait on the sidings. In wintertime, shaven-headed village kids practice controlled skids at the bus turnaround. There's a smell of coal smoke in the air. The waiting room has painted paneling and a tiled stove. The window of the ticket office is barred. The train for Budapest leaves at 12:42 A.M. It stops for a minute and then vanishes like a specter. The station's deserted at that hour. When it rains, the lights from the signals are reflected on the wet platforms and creep along the glistening tracks. One summer, near the station I saw two cows harnessed to a wagon with iron wheels. A fat old woman was walking alongside. In the evenings, especially on Fridays and Saturdays, bands of drunk and dismal youths in hoods and wide pants appear. They try to curse as loud as possible, but they lack the strength. Their jackets and sweatshirts bear inscriptions they do not understand, and when they're alone they whisper these quietly to themselves like rosaries or magic spells. But now, as they strive to swear at the top of their voices, the railroad police come along in their field uniforms with guns and nightsticks. They're over forty and beginning to feel old. The shaven-headed kids remind them of their sons, so they shoo them resignedly onto the dark square in front of the station and tell them to go back to their homes, to their country cottages with their harnessed cows; they tell them to go back to the world they so desperately want to escape in their sweatshirts with incomprehensible slogans. On the square in front of the station there's a parking lot. At the end of the week, after ten in the evening, the lot is filled with cars waiting for the train from Warsaw. The men are coming home from the building sites of the capital. On Sunday afternoon they go back. Now they're saying their loud hellos, throwing their bags of dirty laundry onto the back seat and getting in next to their wives or their brothers. The restrooms are open, but at this time no one's guarding them or taking fifty groszy for use of the urinal. The window of the currency exchange bureau is covered with a white curtain. I'm describing all this because I want to be done with my story already. People sit in the cafeteria or the waiting room, or stroll along the platforms, but it all looks as if the tracks ended here. The little mongrel continues to yap at passengers, and the cars of the Budapest train pass through like phantoms; no one's ever seen anyone getting into them at eighteen minutes to one in the morning, or getting out at 4:17 A.M. Sometimes I see people sleeping. They're dozing, waiting for the dawn, for some local connection to Jasło or Biecz. They have plastic bags under their arms. They look as if they'd just intended to step out of their homes for a minute, as if the night has taken them by surprise. They hardly ever have any luggage, yet they're as tired as if they'd traveled the length and breadth of the country. They're mostly men, in cheap clothes and dust-covered shoes. They take shelter in their leather jackets like turtles in their shells, conserving the dwindling warmth, and rest their heads on the plastic tabletops. Their smell mingles with the smell of food, and the cafeteria acquires the scent of a cold house. At one time there was the pinball machine, but now all is quiet. You can get a decent meal for three or four zlotys. Though the coffee is lousy. The chairs are made of shining aluminum, and the plates, knives, and forks are plastic. Sometimes the railroad men swap their meal tokens for chocolate. I'm describing all this because no one else will. One time, in the late evening, I saw a father and son. The boy must have been around ten or eleven. They were sitting at a bare table. They had a bag with them. The man was drab and small. He looked old and he could've been the boy's grandfather, except that I heard the kid call him "dad." Though perhaps it wasn't age but exhaustion. They didn't resemble one another. It looked as though they were sitting together by accident. The father came from some ancient time, from some remote place. He sat on his cafeteria chair, awkward, made uncomfortable by all the light and the presence of other people. I sensed he would gladly have hidden in the shadows of the station, somewhere on the platform; but it was cold and frosty outside. He placed his large work-worn hands on the table but then, shocked by their appearance and their inactivity, hid them under the tabletop and folded them on his lap. In the meantime his son wriggled and turned, leaning this way and that, yawning, ostentatiously bored. His outfit—jacket, cap, pants—was brightly colored. His father's clothing lacked any noticeable color. Dark blue, gray, maybe faded black—in any case, something that space absorbs without any difficulty. In the plastic, gray and white, sterile decor of the cafeteria, the man looked naked and defenseless, whereas his son was untouched. Wrapped in colors and slogans, he felt at home. He was unaffected by the world, or by the gaze of the other passengers. I imagined taking a picture of them, and then, years later, someone looking at it.

Outside the Gas Station

A while back, in a Polish magazine I read a report about Saturday-night discotheques in the villages. In the dark of night these places look like stray fragments of Las Vegas, shards of a universal temple of delights, like Caligula's Rome with electricity—the multicolored lights entice, tempt, and promise. Young ladies of sixteen are skimpily, provocatively dressed. They look as if they were trying at any cost to jump out of their minuscule outfits. When the bathroom's busy they simply squat nearby and pee, waving to the photographer who's taking their picture. Their boys wear tight-fitting clothing in accordance with the latest trends, as shown on MTV. And, as you might expect at a discotheque, they've had a little to drink, and they're looking to act out scenes from an American action movie. Most of them are skinny with protruding ears: the fashion of recent years, which has them shave their heads completely, exposes them mercilessly. Drug dealers circulate among the village kids offering marihuana, Ecstasy, and amphetamines. The music pounds, the bass vibrates in their arteries, the pulse of the rhythm matches the rhythm of the Ecstasy and the rhythm of their hearts. Some of them simply pass out after seven hours of dancing and fun. At such times the organizers call for an ambulance.

The dawn is pitiless. Saturday night is over and there's no Vegas, there's no Caligula; the lights have been turned off. All around there are gray, stone-built houses, while further away, beyond the village, fields of beet and rye and potato can be seen. You can hear the barking of dogs and the ringing of the bell summoning the faithful to morning mass. It's mostly elderly women who go to church so early in the morning. They pass the last cars that no one had the energy to start up. They pass the bodies of their grandsons and granddaughters lying somewhere in the ditches and bushes. In black dresses, with dark floral scarves on their heads, with old-fashioned handbags and prayer books, they look as if they'd only just left the nineteenth century—while what they happen to see in the street presages a demonic tomorrow. Images from television—reports from distant, strange, and savage lands about remorseless hedonism and instant gratification at any price—are beginning to come to life.

The bus arrives four times a day. Winter lasts four months. Hardly anyone believes in the reality of their own lives, because no one believes those lives will ever be shown on television. Young people think only about getting away, both from the place and the time they were born into. Adults and the elderly have all joined the cult of the past: once, everything was better. The present is something like a curse.

The migration of peoples—in which, by now, we all participate—is basically just an immense form of escape. We run away, we emigrate from the space that till now has been ours, from our own history, from our own lives. There was a time when we set out on these journeys in order to make our lives more valuable, fuller, better—larger and more human. Now, however, as we live, we seek at any cost to abandon our lives entirely, to leave them behind; we wish to become someone else, all at once. In the culture of the West these processes are already familiar, and resemble a game more than a drama. One can choose a personality, a temperament, a worldview, the same way one chooses a place to live. Freedom of choice is an everyday matter. Personality is changed like the color of one's hair.

Here, "east of the West," everything comes into sharper focus. The game turns imperceptibly into the drama. The girls and boys I was trying to describe make no choices. They're attempting to change their lives instantaneously, out of desperation. They're attempting to escape their own existence, at all costs, because it seems to them that whatever happens to them, it'll be better than the lot they were born to. In a way, they're like Indians encountering the civilization of the white invaders, and like the Indians they die of unfamiliar illnesses and an inept use of alcohol. From the civilization of the West, they've taken only remnants and its trash. Because remnants and trash happen to be what's most available. The primitive, vulgar offerings of pop culture encounter a particular sort of vacuum here in the east of Europe. Here, history uprooted entire nations and generations. The twentieth century constituted an interruption in cultural continuity. It may be that this gap was never entirely filled. An inhabitant of this part of the world looks back and sees the last few decades as a series of defeats, betrayals, and bloody experiments performed on the living organisms of societies. He looks back and doesn't find anything he can lean on. The past has been stolen, tarnished, ransacked. The most that can be salvaged from it are legends, myths, or anachronistic ideals that elsewhere have fallen out of usage. Yes indeed, the twentieth century was a write-off, with the exception of its final decade.

Yet, what's ten years of one century and the first five of the next? Identity can't be reconstructed in such a short time. We emerged from nonexistence before we were able to find ourselves a form, a character, an identity precisely; but it turned out that we didn't need to do even this. It's enough to take on the grotesque gestures of contemporary mass culture for us to be instantly absorbed into the universal community of individuals living, playing, suffering, and experiencing emotions all in exactly the same way.

In the main town of my county there's a large gas station. In the evenings, especially on Fridays and Saturdays, young people meet there. In front of the station, which has a store and a café, there are often several dozen cars parked. These vehicles are a big symbol of European integration. All of them were previously driven by citizens of "old Europe." Since May 2004, two million used cars have been imported into my homeland. Mostly from Germany, and mostly Volkswagen Golfs. Now these Golfs are parked in front of the gas station in my county town. Some have their engines on, because it's cold, and in many of them the bass is thumping. Inside them, life is being lived—hurriedly, because the weekend is short. The young drivers of many of the cars can still remember traveling by horse-drawn cart. The bass speakers drown out the past and efface it.

In the shadow of the gas station the young people make love, drink, and do business. You can hear shouts, curses, sometimes the sound of breaking glass. Occasionally a police car appears and for a moment there's calm. Then the police drive off and the party starts up again. Someone throws up, someone cuddles someone else, someone goes into the store for another can of beer. Groups move from one car to another. It's a little like a caravan encampment where cars play the roles of both horses and tents. From time to time someone drives off and a short while later returns. Because these young people have cars, but they don't have anywhere to travel to in them. Or perhaps it just doesn't occur to them that they could actually go somewhere.

Whenever I visit this station of mine on a Friday or Saturday evening, I can't shake off the impression that I'm among emigrants. These young people really look as if they don't have anyplace to go. They meet in this trashy, cold, unwelcoming, alien place, which itself is a symbol of loneliness and estrangement. No one wants to stay at a gas station any longer than necessary. No one who doesn't have to. A gas station is homelessness incarnate. And that's why these boys and girls look like emigrants in their own country. They gather in this cold place to show one another their used cars imported from Germany. It's quite possible that their true homeland is a Volkswagen Golf III.

Perhaps this is what the future will look like. Our homelands, our countries, will vanish, as mental or cultural points of reference. Poland will disappear, Italy will disappear, France will disappear. Why not? More and more things are disappearing and more and more new ones are emerging in their stead. What will remain is Fiat, Coca-Cola, Microsoft, Nike, and Johnny Walker. Then Fiat and Ford will disappear too, even Nokia will disappear, and their more perfect future incarnations will arrive, to which we will pray in turn for consolation and hope.

It's entirely likely that in such a way the West will finally join with the East. The homelessness of all the mental emigrants will in the end become our common home.

The Space of Freedom

In Lubljana, on Metelkova Street, there's a hotel, or rather a youth hostel. Immediately beyond it is a neighborhood of derelict industrial buildings and graffiti-covered squats. Generally speaking, it's a really artsy, "alternative" part of town. That's what the hotel flyers claim, anyway. Once there was a garden-variety prison here. Actually, the high wall topped with barbwire is still standing. All that's missing are watchtowers. The concrete yard is littered with trash and makes a rather agreeable impression. Across from the hostel building is a junk-filled lot with disused shops, an abandoned World War II jeep, and an improvised open-air bar for squatters, now deserted and quiet. Here too the dominant mood is one of tranquil decline: someone has left a handful of sculptures made of old welded bicycle parts and pieces of pink plastic glued together. Metal barrels stand around along with machine parts—in other words, avant-garde art mingling with bygone technology—and no one worries especially about the one or the other.

It's not far to the train station, the bus station, and to Lubljana's beautiful fairy-tale downtown. I was at the hotel in

March, and they were overbooked. In the bar downstairs an international crowd sat drinking beer. You had to take off your shoes before entering the "Café Oriental" and sitting on cushions, though on the plus side there was a hookah in the corner. When you left you had to turn in your bed linen personally, and then they returned your ten-euro deposit. The price of a room included a modest but tasty breakfast. On the first night a band of black drummers from France turned up. Their ramshackle old bus barely made it through the narrow streets. Half a dozen mongrel dogs came with the musicians. One of them spent the night in the bus. I saw it in the morning, sitting proudly in the driver's seat and looking down on the Slovenes hurrying to work. The previous evening I was a little worried the drummers would put on a concert somewhere in the depths of the hostel. I was afraid because the building was exceptionally resonant. In prisons, especially old ones, it's often the case that echoes travel their interiors as easily as drafts.

It was an old slammer from the Austro-Hungarian days. It functioned perfectly well right up until the breakup of Yugoslavia: it was democracy that finally broke its "teeth of bars," as Jacek Kaczmarski's song puts it. Only metaphorically, as it happens—with an eye to the international clientele, the windows are still barred. In the 1990s someone bought the derelict building and renovated it. They invited artists from all over the world to decorate the interior with their graphical and architectural visions. *Never ever prison again! The space of freedom with the inspiration of youth!*—this was the slogan thought up by the initiators of the project.

On the walls of my room, that is to say my cell, an artist had painted rather indistinct but anatomically accurate figures of women. They were probably meant to be the prisoners' dreams. The aerodynamic women were accompanied by the lyrics of the Leonard Cohen song "Tower of Love." The room was cramped as hell—it was filled with steel constructions, ladders, and illuminated canvas screens with paintings in pastel colors. In a cell that had been intended to hold four criminals, two people could barely move around now. You had to step cautiously, like a spy, so as not to damage the art. In addition to the steel door onto the hallway, the room was also guarded by a metal grille. The hotel staff suggested that the door be left open and only the grille be locked, so all the guests could enjoy the interiors of each other's rooms. A beautiful idea, I thought to myself.

In the night, voices reverberated in the hallway like in a well. I heard people conversing in many European languages. Lovers whispered to one another in Croatian, German, and Portuguese, but they sounded as if they were hooked up to an amplifier. It reminded me of the nighttime sounds of real prisoners I'd once listened to. The guards wore felt-bottomed shoes, but even so they deprived the inmates of sleep. To be honest, I wasn't exactly thrilled by all this. I couldn't sleep, and

I felt that here, popular culture was trying to assimilate—with unthinking relish—something ambiguous, repulsive, and obscene. The filth, the stench, the humiliation, the loneliness, and the profanity of a prison—all were transformed via the touch of a magic wand into "the space of freedom," for the price of twenty euros per person for a double cell and fifteen for a triple.

The cells had no bathrooms. The bathrooms were down the hall, right next to the "point of peace"—a room for meditation, prayer, and contemplation. I got up early in the morning to avoid the rush. But I wasn't the first. Standing in front of one mirror was a kid resembling a stock Italian from television; he splashed water on his hair, combed it, and checked the effect a dozen times. At the other mirror, a slightly older youth who looked like an American from a gangster movie was shaving with an electric razor, working with great precision to leave only a thin black strip of beard and moustache. As I took my shower and brushed my teeth, next to them I felt like a country bumpkin.

At breakfast there was an English-speaking family at the next table. The boy of eight or nine whispered to his forty-year-old father: "Daddy, is this a real prison?"

Yes, son. As real as they come.

Banknotes

I've been around for over forty years, and I remember a lot of different kinds of banknotes: for example, the red hundred-zloty bill with a portrait of a worker on the front. On the other side was a picture of a factory that was supposed to be an allegory for industrialization in general. A dozen chimneys spewing smoke into the sky, a black locomotive rumbling along in a cloud of white steam, stacked buildings like relics of nineteenth-century industrial architecture or the metaphysical landscapes of Giorgio de Chirico. Its revolutionary red color was suffused with a strange, unsettling glow, as if the scenes it depicted were taking place in some proletarian underworld.

This is the banknote I remember the best, because at the time my father worked in a factory. Throughout the 1960s he would bring home a wad of these red bills and hand them over to my mother. My child's mind imagined that the factory paid him for his work with its own likeness.

On the steel-blue twenty there was a countrywoman in a headscarf. On one side of the green fifty you could see the head of a fisherman, and on the other a port, cranes, and ships that looked like children's toys. The brown five hundred had miners. They were digging coal from a dark crater with pickaxes and spades.

The socialist-realist style was abandoned for the thousand-zloty bill, which appeared much later. It bore a picture of Nicholas Copernicus and a zodiacal map of the sky. This note had no association with exertion, with a reward for hard work. It was an abstract composition intended to serve as a reminder that money is merely a conventional thing. In any case, my mother didn't like the thousand-zloty bill. She didn't really believe you could buy anything with it.

Alongside all this, of course, there were American dollars. First illegally, on the black market, then under the official gaze of the authorities, who finally if reluctantly accepted reality. The dollar was a second, alternative and, it goes without saying, much more dependable currency. It was hoarded by rural Poland and speculated in by the underground currency markets of the cities. The green images of American presidents were accumulated in out-of-the-way villages, buried in glass jars along with gold rubles from czarist times, tucked behind religious pictures and in other safe places for fear of mice, fire, and thieves. After all, the overwhelming majority of those who had emigrated to America were inhabitants of the poorest rural regions of Poland, and they never broke their ties with their families back home.

In the mid-1970s, the representations of working people disappeared never to return, along with their monochromatic coloring. They were replaced by heroes of the national pantheon in ever-brighter hues. This, it would seem, was the first sign of the end of communism, which had now been forced to appeal to kings from a thousand years ago: that is to say, out-and-out representatives of the feudal system, or to Frederick Chopin, who played for the bourgeoisie and aristocracy of Paris. Yet the worst was yet to come: the denominations began to grow bigger. Ten thousand, twenty thousand, fifty thousand . . . The first "democratic" bill from 1990 was already a hundred thousand, then five hundred thousand, a million, and finally things stopped at two million. The patrons of this inflationary series were of course artists and writers. In my part of the world, when times are uncertain we usually turn to culture, since it's a domain whose failures are not so glaring as those of economics and politics.

Now, with the zloty stabilized, our banknotes once again feature kings whose reigns are remembered well, while the denominations begin with a modest ten zlotys and rise to a moderate hundred.

I gaze at the banknotes of the euro and I wonder to myself what story we'll be able to tell with them. I wonder what tale they'll convey, for example, to the inhabitants of my village. How will the villagers read those windows and bridges remote in time and space—all that Gothic, Renaissance, baroque, and Secession architecture, in misty pastel shades? The notes bear no human faces; there's nothing on them that could be associated with life. Well, except for the numbers—except for the denominations. So it's only going to be those twenties, fifties, and hundreds that stir the imagination and enliven our memories, triggering the game of incessant comparisons and calculations. The past, instead of telling some kind of story, will become a space for computations, the domain of bookkeeping.

For many people the outline of Europe is a fiction, or something like superfluous information taken from a geography lesson and instantly forgotten because it isn't needed (and besides, what kind of outline is it that sentences two thirds of Ukraine to nonexistence . . .).

These banknotes with their wan universal beauty will render money an abstract value divorced from reality, from the concreteness of labor, from the exchange of actual goods and services. In a certain sense, they tell us the future of our continent, and perhaps also the future of the western world. After all, money already serves a function diametrically opposed to what it had been used for till recently: farmers are paid *not* to produce as much as they can, that is to say, people are given money for desisting from work. Who knows if that isn't what our future will look like: we'll receive phantom money for refraining from producing things that no one wants.

Mid-October, Return

At eight in the morning it's quiet and white. Then the mist gradually rises and a diffuse golden light appears. Bushes and trees in the yard come into view, then the fence and the rest of the scenery slowly resume their places. The hoarfrost vanishes from the grass. Silvery spider's webs glisten on the branches. But it's still quiet—quiet and cold. Individual drips can be heard falling from the north side of the roof into the guttering.

This is autumn, mid-October. Some of the trees—alder and ash—have already partly lost their leaves; the familiar landscape is suddenly changing, and new vistas open up in unexpected places. The eye encounters no resistance and enters the heart of the landscape. Amid the leafless branches abandoned birds' nests can be seen. One day, skeins of wild geese appear in the sky, flying south. In the evening, the sound of sheepbells can be heard. The highlanders are bringing their flocks down from the Bieszczady Mountains, and they pass through my village on their way to the lower hills of Podhale. The journey will take them ten days.

Every morning I go out onto the terrace and watch the mist rising. The sun appears, and the trees ignite with red and gold flames. There is no light more beautiful than the light of fall. In the still air, the glow effaces the outline of things, leaving only colors. Even sounds are clearer; they're distinct from one another and last longer. Down below, in the village, someone is chopping wood. I can hear the individual blows of the axe and the thud of the cut logs falling on the pile. This is how things are in the morning, because later in the day the air fills with noises: a tractor drives by; a saw is heard in the woods; a few kilometers away a motorcycle whines up a steep slope; a rooster crows; there's a rustle of falling leaves. The glow and the quiet seem somehow inevitable. This is the true end of the seasons, the end of life, and, if we're lucky or are granted grace, this is what our own end will look like. I think these things to myself as I stand on the terrace and gaze into the fiery infinity of an October day.

A couple of days ago I was driving through southeastern Poland, first along the Vistula through Wilga and Maciejowice. Over and again the river bottoms to my right reflected the gold and blue glow of the sky. Cows were standing on the low meadows, yet they weren't grazing but merely looking ahead into the luminous emptiness, into the dying green of autumn, into their bovine oblivion.

In Puławy I crossed to the other side of the river. I wanted to visit Janowiec. I'd always seen the ruins from the far bank. On Mondays the museum was closed. I didn't meet a living soul, either on the escarpment, or in the grounds, or by the manor house. Skeletons of old boats laid out as exhibits shone a ruddy color in the sun, like children's toys whittled from fresh bark. The ravine at the foot of the castle walls recalled a charcoal kiln. A blue mist hung over the river and I couldn't see Kazimierz. I drove down the hill, passed slowly through the village, and found the road to the ferry. But the ferry wasn't operating. The guy at the landing shrugged helplessly and said it was engine trouble, that it had been three days. He couldn't remember where the nearest other crossing was upstream. I didn't want to risk it, so I went back to Puławy to take the old road through Kazimierz and Opole Lubelskie.

And everywhere it was the same; everywhere there was the same frenzied carnival, the same dance on the volcano's rim, everywhere the plumes of fire and sulfur, as if the world were about to explode, to turn into sparks and flaming fragments and vanish forever into the cold dark abyss of space. Such were my thoughts; I can't help it. I was driving as if in a dream, and I'm not at all sure the wheels of the car were even touching the asphalt. In Józefowa the road again attached itself to the river. Poplars loomed on the right, while sandy pastures extended down toward the water. Houses stood on the left. Old women in headscarves sat on benches warming themselves in the last sunlight. It was just like a hundred or even two hundred years ago, the same sun falling on the same landscape.

So I drove and asked myself: Is this still my country, or have I found myself abroad, crossing some divine Checkpoint

Charlie and emerging on the far side of the invisible window of the world? Somewhere beyond Dębica I began to drift left, toward the east, because I always drift toward that part of the world, toward the Dynów and Strzyżów Hills, toward the hollows amid high ground, those narrow places in the landscape inhabited by forgotten people leading inconspicuous lives. I entered this scenery of decaying matter, old age, fruitless effort, huts, sheds, tiny cottages, crumbling brick, smoldering wood, the heroic struggle to survive, this Poland of villages and hamlets, with three buses a day and ancient asphalt that will be there forever. But in the supernatural autumn light it all looked as though it were about to ascend into heaven, as though it had only been pausing here temporarily, perching like a bird of paradise, and was just about to fly off to the heavens again, leaving the burned, dead earth behind. Such were my thoughts near Hłudne and Wesoła and Barycz. And I felt again that the car's wheels were barely touching the patched asphalt. Afternoon was gradually coming and the light was growing denser, turning into liquid honey, into the gleam that can be seen in old icons. The only difference was that in icons there are no shadows, because icons are meant to depict heaven itself. Whereas by the time I reached Domaradz, the shadows were already twice as long as the objects they belonged to.

And I think to myself that this country of mine—melancholy, mediocre, beautiful and hopeless, despairing and painfully banal, sublime and comic, gray as a mouse, drab as rain, and melancholically ordinary—once a year, at this very time and in this kind of autumn, is accorded something like grace, and all its sins are cleansed.

Amen, dear friends, amen.

All Souls' Day

On All Souls' Day, a journey across Poland resembles a fairy tale or a dream. Fires burn in the darkness. On hills, outside the town limits, in black wildernesses, suspended in the depths of night like twinkling magic carpets, like fiery mirages, like apparitions woven from tiny red and gold and green flames, cemeteries come to life. Over the largest ones there is a glow and a cloud of black kerosene smoke. Cities are filled with the smell of burning funerary candles. It's a strange, anachronistic holiday. It doesn't belong in our era. It turns attention away from the practical and the everyday. Thousands, tens of thousands, hundreds of thousands of us lose precious time traveling the length and breadth of the country to visit remains buried in the ground—what's left of those who once were with us. It's a tribal, barbarian holiday. Our memory is not enough. We have to feel our dead physically; we have to know that they lie six feet below us and are gradually turning to earth, breaking down into their constituent parts and becoming minerals. And all this takes place amid evening fires and columns of black smoke.

The pagan, pre-Christian cult of the ancestors has endured. It may be the third most important holiday in our calendar, after Easter and Christmas. In addition, it's the only one of the three that has resisted commercialization, has resisted being tamed and degraded into an empty ceremony, to a family rite at a table piled with food. The dead allow us to recover part of our lost humanity. Once a year we become religious in the simplest, most archaic way, and we regress to the days when we began to be aware of our own humanity. In silence and solitude we go to where the bodies of our loved ones lie—the bodies from which we ourselves have come. We visit our own past buried in the ground. It could be said that this ritual is a recollection of religiousness from a time before the arrival of God, when we paid tribute to something greater than us—our own history enclosed in the bodies of our forebears.

Fires burn on graves. From above, from the sky, in the darkness they must look like encampments, temporary towns, or frozen torch-lit processions. Once a year we mark with fire the places where we've buried our dead, so that they might abide forever, so that they can be visited, so that they can be found. No one testifies to our own existence better than them. What would humankind be without ancestors? It's an absurd question. So then, once a year we mark those places with lights so that the dark, empty, uninhabited, and boundless reaches of space should know we're engaged in a battle with them, a battle with their nothingness, their indifference. That's why the fires burn. At dusk everyone leaves, climbs into their cars and buses and goes back home. The cemeteries are left deserted and illuminated. It's one of the most captivating sights to be seen in Poland. This image says more about us than we ourselves are capable of expressing or comprehending.

My own loved ones do not lie here where I live. But there are cemeteries everywhere in the area. There are Lemko graveyards—all that remains of the villages resettled in the 1940s. There are Austro-Hungarian military cemeteries, a memento of the First World War and the Battle of Gorlice-Tarnów, one of the bloodiest encounters of that period. In the immediate vicinity, within four or five miles, I have maybe ten such cemeteries. I say "I have" because for several years now I've tried to visit all of them around All Souls' Day. Some of them lie in remote places, in abandoned valleys where there once were villages. So I arrive, light candles, and read out the names written in Cyrillic script. Because this is the only way we can stop someone from dying for good: saying their name without even knowing their face. That's the only thing that can be done. To speak sounds out loud that are forever linked to someone's life. Sometimes there's already a candle or two here and there. Someone came here, visited, but then disappeared, as if they themselves were a ghost.

The soldiers' graves often lack a name. The nameplates have gotten lost or been destroyed by rust; the wind and rain have completely eaten away the enameled lettering. But the Austro-Hungarian bureaucracy and its archives were excellent guardians of memory, and thanks to them we know that in the cemetery at Lipna lies Franz Soliwarz of the 47th Infantry Regiment, Franz Kocbek of the same unit, and three of their comrades. From the 14th Fusilier Regiment as many as twelve men are to be found here, including Johann Červeny, Gottlob Odvárka, and Anton Trkan—may they rest in peace.

And so I visit a dead army and the former inhabitants of nonexistent villages. Sometimes the dusk finds me still there, and I return in the dark. In places, isolated flames are burning. In the absolute darkness they look like will-o'-the-wisps luring travelers to their doom. And in a certain sense that's how it should be on the Day of All Souls—this day ought to knock us off balance and take away our reason, so that—if only for a moment—we can believe in the immortality of those whose ashes we walk upon. And, at the same time, to believe at least a little in our own.

Will-o'-the-Wisps of the Dead

It can best be seen at the beginning of November. Funerary candles burn in abandoned valleys. The wind carries the smell of stearin. I have no idea who lights those candles. When I come there on the first or second of November with my family, they're already lit. In Czarne, in Długie, in Radoczyn, which stretches all the way to the Slovak border. In each cemetery there are two or three small flames in soot-blackened glass jars, contending with the wind. It's hard to get here; no one lives in these places anymore. The villages were once Ukrainian, or more precisely Lemko. Between 1945 and 1947, the communists resettled them, just like that. Partly in the Soviet Union and partly in western Poland, from which the Germans had already been expelled. It was a distant and relatively weak echo of the great Stalinist deportations.

Hence the emptiness of the landscape. You can spend an entire day wandering the mountain valleys and encounter only cemeteries or what's left of them. Austrian cemeteries from the First World War are often located in the vicinity of Ukrainian ones, either Uniate or Orthodox. Both the one and the other are like signs of some ancient forgotten civilization. In the summer they simply disappear under luxuriant greenery and tall grass, in the shade of lofty trees; it's only the nakedness of November that lends them a hyperreal distinctness.

At dusk, in the encroaching darkness, in the blue autumn mist, small yellow or red lights are burning. You drive cautiously down a gravel road or a dirt track and every mile or two there glimmers a will-o'-the-wisp of the dead, while all around there's no sign of a living soul, no house, nothing. Yet someone lights those lamps on the tombs of soldiers from ninety years ago. Most of the graves no longer have inscriptions. Some cemeteries consist of no more than traces or fragments. But even in the ones that have been restored, the fallen lie nameless. It's only in documents preserved in the archives of Vienna and Kraków that you can find names: Antoni Nemec, Franciszek Kladnik, Jan Schweringer, Mateus Cepuš, Gottlieb Kyselka, Artur Böhm, Leib Issman, Sándor Szasl, Josef Dymeček, Jan Kocanda, Adolf Angst, Emil Husejnagič, Hakija Gjukič, Tadeusz Michalski, Petro Santoni, Batto Delazer, Andre Stefančič, Feliks Conti, Hatko Podlegar . . .

So I light my own candles and read the names, and then I go back home. Of course, their families remember them, but here, where they perished, hardly anyone knows their names. This is my own private rite, a quiet mass and a pagan lighting of fires for the dead at the beginning of November.

It was through this region that the Russians tried to force their way across the Carpathian mountain passes in the winter of 1914. If they'd succeeded, the Hungarian Plain, Budapest, and Vienna would have been within their reach, and who knows how the world would look today . . . Fortunately, things worked out otherwise, and now I can imagine the Russian infantry in their gray greatcoats plodding through the snow toward the low passes in Radoczyn or Konieczna. On their backs they carry rolled-up blankets, while on their gun barrels there are bayonets like long skewers, which are only good for stabbing—not, as in the case of Austrian or Prussian bayonets, for cutting bread and opening cans. The buildings in the villages have burned down and there's no shelter. They have to wade through deep snow under fire from the mountain artillery and from Schwarzlose and Maxim machine guns. The world has three colors: the white of the snow, the muddy brown of the earth torn up by shells, and the red of blood. When I look at old black-and-white photographs, the red is the only thing missing. The rest is there. Everything is monochromatic, dull gray, wallowing in mud, leafless. The soldiers live in foxholes, bivvies, and tattered tents; their life resembles a gypsy caravan or a refugee camp, the only difference being that they are under constant threat of death.

I find these old photographs in the museum in my nearby county town. This small museum is supposed to present the long, rich, complex history of the entire region. But half its exhibits concern the story of a few months in 1914 and 1915. Half its exhibits are about the First World War. Next to these few wartime months, the rest of that long and complicated history seems nothing more than a brief interlude. This aside, there's building work going on in the cellars, and when I asked what was being added, the director said: a wax museum, which will include the figures of the Emperor Franz Joseph, the Good Soldier Švejk, the most important commanders of the campaign on the Austro-Hungarian, Prussian, and Russian sides, and a single Pole who commanded an infantry regiment.

And so it seems as if the First World War, and really only one chapter of it, was the most important thing to have taken place in my part of the world. You could say it's the only event of world significance that it was our lot to experience, here in the southeastern portion of my country. True, at the time this country didn't even exist on maps, and was divided between three empires; but in some way it still managed to take part in the European and global game. After all, the First World War was in a certain sense a cosmopolitan war. At least from the Austro-Hungarian perspective. Who knows if the fondness for those times, and the special memory of that war, doesn't arise out of nostalgia for a period in which a person's own individual identity was, quite naturally, a part of a larger universal reality. It's quite possible that the "prison of nations," as the Austro-Hungarian Empire was called back then, will come in time to be seen as a kind of prototype, however imperfect, of a unified Europe. Such a view is of course naïve and sentimental. Still, precisely here—in southern Poland, in Galicia, in the former Austro-Hungarian partition—the conviction that the First World War was also "our" war runs quite deep. Just like the conviction that Franz Joseph was "our" emperor. Kaiser Wilhelm could never have dreamed of such a thing, not to mention Czar Nicholas.

I also have the impression that the image of the First World War in Galicia yielded rather easily to aestheticization. No doubt because it was the last war of the old variety. Here no one used gas, there were no tanks, and the fighting never took on the ghastly character of trench warfare. All that was the lot of the Western front. It was there that techniques of mass slaughter were tested out; there that soldiers found themselves in muddy earthworks for months on end, among rats and the decaying corpses of their comrades in arms. In comparison with Verdun and the Somme, the war here in the East followed a rather old-fashioned and dignified course. In the black-and-white photographs from those days you can see a calm, almost idyllic landscape: snow-covered hills, leafless stands of trees, white rooftops, smoke rising from chimneys. Amid this scenery the small figures of the soldiers and the outlines of horse-drawn carts look like everyday village bustle; the pictures give off an atmosphere such as might be found in the paintings of Pieter Brueghel, for example *Hunters in the Snow*. Next to this, the bloody plains of northern France, strewn with putrefying flesh, seem like a hell of modern annihilation. In the West, the twentieth century was beginning, whereas here, in Galicia, it was still the nineteenth, as Cossack divisions fought with regiments of hussars and uhlans. The Austro-Hungarian top brass issued orders specifying that soldiers, especially officers, were to assume "fighting poses" when being photographed. And just such a "fighting" mien is demonstrated by Lieutenant Colonel Ernest Pittl, commander of the IV Battalion's 100th Infantry Regiment: his moustache bristles, he holds a revolver in his right hand while his left is stretched out, as if pointing to the enemy, and his steady and pitiless gaze is fixed on the camera. Yes, this war had something of the theater, of a stage production, about it. After all, Švejk observed it like some kind of immense cabaret, a universal vaudeville and a foreshadowing of the theater of the absurd. And Švejk fought in Galicia. I'm trying to imagine what would've happened if by some miracle he had found himself on the Western Front in the capacity, say, of Ernst Jünger's orderly. With an orderly like that, recounting his endless preposterous anecdotes, would Jünger still have had the courage to write *Storm of Steel*? Would he have had the strength to take on the pathos and gravity of his own story? Whereas, would Hašek's Švejk have been possible in the mud of Flanders, stinking of human carrion? Wouldn't it all have simply deprived him of the power of speech—wouldn't he have descended into madness? Because the Western Front was a glimpse into the future of Europe. In Galicia, war was still waged in the old style, though Švejk could already sense the menace and horror of history to come. Where Jünger saw heroism and a change in the paradigms of reality, Švejk perceived only farcicality and the unthinking belly laugh of the world.

I'm writing so much about Švejk, about a fictional character, because in these parts the First World War—or rather, the memory of that war—bears his face. He's a Czech hero, it's true, but in Galicia there are all kinds of statues or small images of him in different towns, pubs often bear his name, and his likeness hangs in noisy smoke-filled beer halls; one could be mistaken for thinking they depict a living person rather than a literary invention. Yes indeed, from that entire war, our most vivid memories are of Franz Joseph and of his most implacable foe, who managed to turn all that was imperial into a grotesque spectacle of political necrophilia and a cabaret of the absurd. Did the First World War produce any other hero of his caliber? No one comes to my mind. Neither Céline's protagonists nor those of Remarque have the vividness of Švejk. They're too preoccupied with themselves, because the war is destroying them. Whereas Švejk with his hypnotic chatter destroys the war. And along the way he destroys the entire meaning and order of the world that existed to that point. Švejk never regrets a thing. He laughs and he dances on graves. He's a nihilist because that's the only way to survive. His creator will finish as a commissar in the Red Army.

Of course, it's not this Švejk who's immortalized in the monuments of Galicia. Here he personifies folksy resourcefulness, good humor, and common sense. More—he represents the thoroughly human, everyday dimension of war—a plebeian adventure that can happen to anyone and that must be gotten through at the least possible cost. To this day, in the military, at least in the Polish army, his memory is alive and his name denotes a soldier who pretends to be incompetent and slow so he'll be left alone and not assigned any complicated or responsible tasks.

It's true, Švejk was a misunderstood visionary. He was a prophet, but in his own part of the world he was taken for a slyboots and a joker. The West was better able to understand his lesson about the destruction of the old world. Here, however, despite everything, attempts were made to save that old world. That's how I'm able to visit those cemeteries of mine in the deserted borderlands between Poland and Slovakia. But not just here. In Galicia as a whole there are more than four hundred of them.

As soon as the gunfire died down in the spring of 1915, when it was already clear who was the victor and who the losers, the Austro-Hungarian high command gave the order to gather together all the fallen, to exhume them from thousands of makeshift burial grounds and individual graves. They were to lie in specially designed necropolises. These were very interesting places, architecturally speaking, often monumental in nature and located far from human habitation, on the tops of mountains. Everyone was buried together, without regard for national identity. Russians lay with Prussians and Austro-

Hungarian citizens. The Orthodox Christians had their three-barred crosses, and the Jews stylized matzevahs with the Star of David. These are often tiny little cemeteries with a single central memorial, nestling by a church cemetery. But you can also find proper monuments, like the cemetery at Łużna, where over a thousand soldiers were buried in specially formed terraces on a hill. Hungarians, Prussians, Russians, and Austrians each lie separately, while from a bird's-eye view the whole resembles the outline of an eagle with wings outspread.

I was there a few days ago. Earlier I'd been looking at photographs of the exhumation of the bodies, their reburial, and the building of the cemetery. Bearded Russian prisoners of war were transporting human remains in wooden containers with handles, two prisoners to each crate. On their sleeves they wore armbands marked with a cross. Their features were Mongol or Tartar. They stared motionless at the camera. They'd come from far away in the dark interior of the Empire, and could scarcely have comprehended all that had happened to them. Above all, they didn't understand the sense behind digging up corpses and moving them from one place to another. This noble, chivalrous gesture must have seemed to them sacrilegious, blasphemous; they must have been frightened of the spirits of the dead. Then, when the remains were interred in their final resting place, those same Russian prisoners of war, skilled in woodwork and carpentry, constructed tall monumental towers called *gontynas* on the lonely hills. They hewed crosses for the graves and made decorative fencing. Italian prisoners, in turn, were put to use in stoneworking. They cut and polished rocks from which they later built walls and gateways with pyramidal towers reminiscent of Babylon or ancient Egypt, just as the wooden monuments recalled pagan temples from some Slavic prehistory. The creators of this whole artistic project, it seems, were seeking to bring it into eternity, to locate it all outside of time. The cemeteries were to remind one of dreams or fairy tales. Just as the First World War today reminds us of a dream or a fairy tale. Or a knightly legend. After everything that came later, after the twentieth century began in earnest, that first worldwide massacre acquired an old-world charm.

Especially here, in Galicia, in the cemetery at Łużna. Though the cemetery chapel lies in ruins, some of the graves have been renovated. They have gleaming new headstones bearing name, rank, and unit. On certain of them, someone has tied ribbons with the Hungarian national colors. Funerary candles flicker in many places. Someone keeps coming here and walking the paths from one sector to another. Someone visits the Russians, the Germans, and the Austrians—which is to say, another dozen or so nationalities aside from those already mentioned: from Bosnians to, for example, Estonians. In the old photographs the cemetery hill is bare. Now it's overgrown with woods, and the hussars, Cossacks, infantry, grenadiers, and all the others lie in the shade of trees.

As I was leaving, an old man came out of a solitary cottage that stood nearby. He smiled and immediately began talking about what his memory held on the subject of the cemetery.

He probably knew all there was to know about the place. He'd been born and brought up in its shadow. He was only ten or fifteen years younger than the graves. He told me that the chapel had burned down in the 1980s, and since that time he'd been afraid of storms. The chapel stood high up, and had a good lightning conductor. But it burned down on a clear day.

I got into my car; he waved goodbye and then walked off among the graves as if he wanted to check whether I'd left everything as it ought to be.

Memory

I remember many places and events. Some of them remain in my memory like characters from a play, frozen. A slight effort is all that's needed to bring them back to life. When this happens, they're illuminated by a strange warm glow that causes the past to come back infinitely diminished, like when you look through the wrong end of a pair of binoculars. The flow of time makes the images smaller but it can't destroy them. They become miniatures of happenings and objects, but they retain their heat, color, and internal sequence. We just have to be bigger than our past in order to retain it.

All these places and events are without exception banal. They could have happened to anyone else and in any other location.

———————

I'm seven or eight years old and it's winter. My father and I are walking down a quiet street in the suburbs of Warsaw. I don't remember how we found ourselves there or why, but I can see very vividly the glassy sidewalk, snow swept into piles, and the white roadway. My father is holding my hand; from time to time I run up and slide on the dark patches of bare ice. Snow lies on the branches of trees and sticks to fences and iron gates. The day is frosty and windless. The air smells of coal smoke. It's the smell of the city's outskirts in those days, when lumbering wagons drawn by hulking draft horses would appear in alleyways. Blackened men in quilted jackets and caps with earflaps would shovel coal into wicker baskets and carry it down into cellars. But on that day the street was completely quiet and deserted. Grayish-yellow smoke rose from chimneys.

This is what life consists of when we try to imagine it to ourselves as a whole—isolated fragments that have stuck in the memory. They're not joined by any logic, any sense, aside from the chance fact that they happened to me.

It's January, seven in the morning, and I've just woken my daughter for school. She's bustling between the bathroom and the kitchen, and I'm sitting in my room drinking coffee and staring out the window. The wintry gray light of early morning brings back all the dawns of my childhood. Many years have gone by; I'm grown up now, my parents are old, and I'm separated from my family home by decades and by hundreds of miles, but the light of dawn hasn't changed in the slightest. I gaze at it and I can recreate the taste of mornings when I was ten. My daughter repeats my gestures, repeats my feelings. When she wakes she stretches reluctantly, rolls up into a ball beneath the quilt and tries to pretend she's only imagining waking up, that in a moment she'll be able to return to the warm embrace of sleep. The coming day is cold and disagreeable, and so the first waking minutes are better imagined as a continuation of the safe, cozy night. You have to go down to the bathroom and the kitchen with half-closed eyes so as to preserve the sleepy stillness for as long as possible. She eats breakfast without speaking and brushes her teeth, and in the meantime I start the car and wait for it to warm up. I watch the front door of the house to capture the moment when she emerges, huddled against the onslaught of the cold wind, and finally sets out to encounter the coming day.

That gentle, fragile continuity of gestures and emotions may well be what gives human life some meaning. It gives meaning to the way we build and decorate successive homes. The rest seems no more than the blind necessity for survival of the species, or an act of vanity.

Aside from places and events, aside from light, there are also objects, the memory of which seems indestructible. For example a clear yellow plastic mug. I've remembered it as my first possession. I was four years old and it appeared in my life as something extremely important. Today, whenever I think "milk" or "sweet tea with lemon" its image immediately appears: a little golden miniature of an adult beer mug. That entire period is enveloped in semi-darkness, plunged in shadow;

it's like a fuzzy black-and-white photograph. Even the faces are indistinct. Furniture in the apartment, fragments of the street and the courtyard, the view from the window—none of it has sharp colors or shapes. By virtue of some bizarre contrast, it's only that child's cup or toy that possesses a clear form and color. It shines like a fairy-tale sun, illuminating the rest of the world of those days with its glow. Out of the gloom it summons the wooden armrests of a chair, the coal-burning kitchen range, and the young face of my father returning from the factory in the late evening.

I'm unable to explain the phenomenon of memory. It probably can't be explained at all, and that's exactly why its clarity vies with its beauty. My mug shines in my past like a star showing me the way. It may be that the recollection of where we come from has to take the simplest form possible, in order that we won't forget it.

I've read thousands of books in my life, I've talked with hundreds of people, made friends with dozens of them; I've seen a lot of the world and been in various strange places. Out of all of this, you'd think some kind of synthesis would arise, some lesson for the future. Yet nothing of the sort has happened. I wake up each morning and wait for events to recede into the past. It's only then that they come into focus, only then that they acquire some meaning. The future is a big vacuum. It contains nothing, and can excite only science fiction fans, Marxists, capitalists, or aging spinsters. Only that which is past exists, because it possesses its own form; it's palpable, tangible, and in a certain sense it saves us from madness, from mental annihilation.

I was in prison once, and during that time I spent a month in solitary confinement. The cell was completely empty; the only personal items I had were an aluminum bowl, plate, and spoon, a toothbrush, and some soap. The whole time I was there I didn't see another human being. Food was pushed in through a small hatch in the door. The toilet and the sink were right there in the cell. I remember it as one of the most interesting times in my life. I experienced total solitude and total abandonment. Of course, I was waiting for it all to end, and I counted the days like any condemned man; but the future didn't really concern me. It was shapeless and abstract. It comprised something like a point on a straight line. What was past, on the other hand, absorbed me. Events from long before came out of the past and filled my head—more, they filled that cramped space so tightly there was no room for either the present or the future. I had the sense that I was entirely self-sufficient and that in essence my freedom had not been taken from me because my memory had not been taken from me. It's entirely possible my life was extended by that month in some inexplicable way, that those thirty days were added to my existence, like a bonus. In the course of four weeks of emptiness and loneliness, everything I had experienced earlier I experienced for a second time. More than that, I experienced it more attentively and with greater susceptibility, so to speak, because I'd begun to understand that you never get anything in life other than what you've already gotten.

That's right. The past and memory are my homeland and my home. I like to get drunk alone and recall past events, people, and landscapes. Even those from a week or two ago. Futurology always repulsed me, because it seemed the result of cowardice, of defection, a betrayal of one's own condition. I never thought of the future as any kind of solution. The future is always the refuge of fools. It arrives, and they have to explain why it didn't arrive the way it was supposed to, or prove that this was exactly what they predicted. That's why I prefer to drink alone or with friends and wait for the past to take us into its possession. It's always better to be with finished beings than potential ones. The past treats us with seriousness, which cannot be said of the future.

"Life is not what one has lived, but what one remembers and how one remembers it" (Gabriel García Márquez). I can't find any better answer to the question of why I am who I am, and where I came from, in this particular place and time. The southern border of Poland, the mountains, January: snow is falling and cutting me off from the rest of the world. Tomorrow morning, driving out in the car will be difficult. Everything arranges itself into a harmonious picture. The surroundings, the winter, the emptiness of the tranquil landscape, the solitude when for days on end I see only my own family. I have the overwhelming impression that everything was planned out long ago, and I'm merely living through variations and sequences of certain primal gestures and events. This may well be a form of fatalism, though I believe rather that in life we repeat, in various forms, all we've remembered. I'm at peace with my lot because in it I perceive continuity. Neither history nor geography is able to guarantee that we'll feel we really come from somewhere. The first is too capricious and unpredictable, the second too indifferent. Besides, both the one and the other serve power, which uses them to try to convince us we owe it something. Memory is independent. It's ruled by its own internal laws of forgetfulness or sudden revelation. Whenever we try to betray it we come out looking pathetic or despicably arrogant. To renounce your memory of yourself is to commit mental suicide. It's enough to look at country folk pretending to be townies, or townies pretending to be aristocracy. They're all fleeing from their own memory and they can't find anything to replace it with. Amnesia is a form of contempt for the self. In the world that's coming we'll have few things of our own. Most of them will be subject to the laws of economy—in other words, every gain will include a potential loss. Probably even feelings will be subject to trade. It'll be possible to buy love and sell hate on a hitherto unknown scale. It's quite likely that only memory—that personal, capricious, and fragmentary history—will find no buyers, because for someone else it will have no value whatsoever.

One time we were driving our ten-year-old daughter to her winter vacation. The closer we got to where she was going to spend the week without us, the more nervous and at the same time the more distant she became. Later, amid the counselors and the other children, the tension grew. We took her bags to her room and wanted to give her a goodbye hug. In the room there was another girl her age. Our daughter's eyes expressed radically contradictory feelings. She wanted us to disappear as quickly as possible, yet at the same time she was sad and hurt that we were going away. Her perplexity and vulnerability were touching. She wanted to break free, to give her life its own shape, yet at the same time memory and the past were forcing her to watch us leave with a sad, apologetic smile on her face.

Our Game of *Bildung*

It's getting on towards midnight, and I'm sitting in the kitchen observing the cultivation of fungus. Thirty years have passed, but in mid-May children in fifth grade still regularly study a chapter entitled "Fungi" in their biology texts. On kitchen windowsills the length and breadth of the country there are saucers with bread crusts covered with a glass or a jar. Delicate white threads slowly take over the container. I have to keep reminding my daughter that fungus doesn't live by bread alone, that from time to time it needs to be given a couple of drops of water. Of course she forgets and I have to feed it myself. I'm experienced in this domain. After all, I grew at least one healthy fungus in my life. It was in May 1972. Of this I'm certain.

I like moving around the house at night and observing how my daughter's life is growing larger. I find opened packets of potato chips, abandoned comic books, school notebooks, video cassettes of Hollywood movies, single shoes, pencil cases, pairs of jeans, hairclips, the remnants of collections of something or other begun and never completed. Unfamiliar cosmetics appear in the bathroom. Disposable jewelry lies scattered in always-unexpected places. The kingdom of toys becomes depopulated, and in its place there appear things that are merely necessary. Instead of cassettes of narrated fairy tales I find tapes of Bob Marley and the Red Hot Chili Peppers. More and more frequently, I notice the scent of perfume in the air, acquired from goodness knows where.

Her world is expanding. It occupies more and more space. Before long it'll stop needing other worlds, or will only need them to a much lesser degree than before. For some time now she's slept with the light off. She doesn't ask us to come into her room and turn off her lamp only once she's properly asleep. She pays less and less attention to her two cats. And more and more to her own reflection in the mirror. With every gesture she tries to set herself apart from the world, to establish an impenetrable boundary between reality and her own existence. This makes me glad and at the same time irritates me. That's probably how things have to be. In a certain sense her gain is my loss.

Her life is now reaching into my past and bringing my own childhood and early youth to the surface. Even if I don't remember my thoughts and feelings, thanks to her I'm able to imagine them, I can recreate their aura. Thanks to her I can escape the rushing torrent of time, because her presence alone gives the lie to transitoriness. She's filled with pure energy that spreads in every direction, hungry to take possession of as much of the world as it can.

The door to her room is closed more and more often. It's only left slightly ajar at night, to let in a sliver of light. For some time now, when I go in to look at her sleeping, I feel like an intruder. Not long ago I did this entirely naturally. The space presented no resistance because it didn't belong to her. Now I have the sense that the dark space is filled with her thoughts and her dreams, which she'll share only when she chooses. At one time I'd go into her room and listen intently and fearfully to see if she was breathing, if her fragile life could contend with the world, the darkness, that immense, infinite expanse surrounding her little bed.

Today it's different. I rest. I'm getting fat. Losing my hair. Ever more frequently, fear perches at the head of my own bed and the immensity of the world deprives me of sleep. The things I want to protect her from are gradually becoming my own problems. She can see this, though she's not able to understand it. She gives a long-suffering sigh and makes scornful faces, while irony and sarcasm creep into her words. She's instinctively seizing the moment when my own strength is abandoning me, while potentiality seethes in her soul and her body.

For some time now, when I'm driving her to school I play Handel or Vivaldi or Bach in the car. I do it for my own pleasure and a little out of contrariness. At these moments she looks at me with studied irritation, raising her eyes to heaven as if complaining to the entire world of the fate that's given her such a hopeless father. She tries to replace the music with her copy of *Legend* or some other idiocy that I myself put her onto a while ago, and that I enjoy listening to myself. Naturally I don't allow her to play it. This is my car, I say, and in it I'll listen to whatever music I like. She pouts furiously and tries to look at herself in the rearview mirror.

A couple of days ago, as we were coming back home, she suddenly broke off the conversation and, as it were absentmindedly, in a trance, she tried to whistle the allegro from "Spring" along with the recording. "What's that?" I asked, feigning surprise. She instantly turned the whole thing into a joke, and started conducting an imaginary orchestra.

That's what our game of *Bildung* looks like. It doesn't exhaust our strength or infringe upon our territories. Well, not to the point of excess.

The Body of the Father

At the beginning of June 1979, for the first time Karol Wojtyła visited Poland as John Paul II. Neither my friends nor I were particularly involved in the life of the Church. Actually, it was quite the opposite. Yet if carnival is a religious experience, then we experienced that moment as a holy time, an upside-down time, a time when time ceased to flow. Such was the spring and summer of 1979. On the streets, in the cafés, in the streetcars you could feel something like a gentle, mind-numbing euphoria. Reality had performed a death-defying somersault and we'd found ourselves in thrall to the surreal. On the one hand dull, dreary communism, the drabness of the everyday, the ugly lifeless faces of apparatchiks on television screens and in the papers, the painful feeling that it would be like this forever, till the end of the world, and that nothing would ever change because the essence of the system was precisely this deadness, immobility, these everlasting death throes. And then, on the other, this unreal, surreal, absurd election of a Pole to St. Peter's Throne. At the time it seemed to us that the whole thing made no sense whatsoever. Someone had played a practical joke on us, someone had turned the world on its head. We were too young and too self-absorbed to comprehend the basic truth about the fact that "The Holy Spirit breathes where it will," and that it had decided for a while—for a split second—to make this strange surreal land on the Vistula River its field of operations. Yes indeed, in the early summer of 1979 we had no notion of such a thing.

We were prowling as usual round the narrow streets of Warsaw's Old Town. It was evening, and the walls and roadways were now yielding up the heat they'd absorbed during the daytime. The following day, on Plac Zwycięstwa, the first papal mass in the country was to be celebrated. That evening the entire Old Town turned into a pedestrian zone. Normally by ten or eleven the place was deserted; on the streets you'd see the last passersby, the last guests from the bars, and the grim specters of uniformed policemen. Now the area between Plac Zamkowy and the Rynek was as full of life as the Corso in some Italian city. Plainclothes security police stood in doorways helplessly watching the crowd flowing by. In normal circumstances they would have checked the ID of the occasional person and told them to be getting home. But they couldn't check the papers of thousands of promenaders.

I believe it was the first sensation of social freedom I can remember in my life. At the time we had long hair and tattered clothes and we took drugs. We formed something of a naive escapist sect. Both the Church and communism seemed to us rather abstract entities. The former was the memory of family oppression in the form of weekly masses and sermons about the flames of hell, which would consume masturbators and other such perverts. The latter persecuted us a little day by day, but for us it had no political, social, historical dimension. I guess we regarded it the way the first Christians regarded the lions and other Roman entertainments. We accepted it as our fate, as a punishment from God, or a natural disaster.

So we could stroll all night, sitting on steps, kissing girls, unafraid of anything. That night was like utopia. I seem to recall there was a ban on alcohol sales in the city at the time, but for sure we had some cheap wine. For sure we kissed girls. Laughter could be heard in the darkness. Couples embraced and sought out secluded places, which were few and far between that evening. We probably treated the whole thing as something of a miracle. For a moment the world, the country, the city, the streets, belonged to us, and we quite simply felt at home. That night we were certain no one would ask us what we were doing there, no one would make suspects of us. The cops stood in gateways and were helpless. The people in uniforms skulked in the shadows almost like we did on ordinary days.

Then, late at night, we went over to Plac Zamkowy, where thousands of people had set up camp so they could wait till morning and take part in the service. I think we had blankets or sleeping bags with us. I remember the pavement was still warm—smooth and warm to the touch like a living body or the sun-heated shell of a primeval creature. Thousands of people were lying or sitting so close they were touching. I lay my head on someone's chest. Some folk were already asleep; some hugged their companion to ward off the chill of night. I wondered what we looked like from above, from high up in the sky. We must have resembled a chaotic pagan tangle of bodies, or a medieval vision of souls being cast into hell on the Day of Judgment. But most of us for sure fell asleep, relaxed by the calm breathing and gentle snores of thousands of people that rose over the square. And that sleeping crowd in the heart of the city was the embodiment of trust. We slept like innocent babes, confident that nothing could happen because a benevolent power was watching over us.

We were woken by the sun. There wasn't an inch of shade on the square. No one went looking for any. In those days there was no mineral water in plastic bottles. We suffered thirst like true pilgrims. We also must have suffered hunger, because no one had gone to the trouble of bringing food. People rubbed their eyes and turned over to try and escape the brightness of day, then in the end they gave up and rose into a sitting position or stood to stretch their limbs. Today I imagine it looked like a kind of resurrection. At the time I probably thought of an immense picnic, something like a rather more serious and lofty Woodstock.

Yet I have no recollection of the moment when John Paul II appeared; I don't remember the Mass or the words he spoke to the crowd. My memory has retained only his white figure at the far end of the square, a long way off. Perhaps his words were not as important as his presence. I suspect, though, that the real miracle of that night and that morning was *our* presence. The real miracle lay in transforming a crowd into a society. After all, he was only doing what he was supposed to—he'd come to us as a priest, a shepherd, and he sought to console us. Whereas we didn't have to listen to him at all. Our response could have been shallow exaltation, national euphoria, a religious elation that was nothing more than sentimentality. We could have left the square with tears in our eyes, temporarily comforted, our spirits raised, and returned to our lives in a slightly better mood, the way a person comes back from a visit to his therapist. It's not so hard to imagine such a turn of events when you think of the pilgrimages John Paul II made to Poland when it was already a free country. At those later times, after all, he was coming to a country that was getting steadily worse from year to year. He celebrated Masses for millions of the faithful, delivered sermons to crowds of hundreds of thousands, traveled the length and breadth of Poland, elevated saints at the altars, blessed people, and left, while the people of God, in response to his teachings about freedom and dignity, allowed the communists to return to power. And then, through some mystical tribal urge, they honored him with dozens of kitschy monuments and named hundreds of streets after him. It was as if during his lifetime they were trying to turn him into an object, a fetish, as if they simply wanted to put him to death, because the demands he made in his teachings were too unreasonable and removed from the everyday. It's easier to blubber a little at a monument than to obey the Ten Commandments—or even five out of ten—for a whole week.

Yet at that time, a miracle happened. A crowd turned into a society, and people realized they weren't a herd but a community. Even us—long-haired, ragged, and up in arms against the whole world—we left that place with the feeling that all those people around us, who looked like our fathers and our mothers and our hated teachers, were, when it came down to it—in some physical, corporeal way—close to us. I remember I felt the touch of foreign bodies and for the first time in my life it wasn't unpleasant, but agreeable in a primal, animal way. It was a little like I'd suddenly understood that, physically, I belonged to humanity—that I was a tiny piece of humankind as a species.

I can't help it—that was the paradoxical feeling I had during a Catholic mass that was supposed to be a spiritual experience.

—————

The next time I saw him was eighteen years later.

He was supposed to come to Dukla. Dukla is two thousand inhabitants in the southeastern corner of Poland. Beyond it there's nothing. I'd shown up there a few hours earlier. A beautiful plebeian holiday was in progress. It was like an immense parish fair. Firemen were on parade in their black and gold dress uniforms, while stern mustachioed policemen in white shirts and light-blue pressed jackets stood on street corners. All around were ranks of stalls with trashy goods—plaster figures of saints, busts of the Pope, bottles of holy water in the shape of the Virgin Mary with a twist-off head, Egyptian dreambooks, an entire trash-heap of disposable toys made of thin plastic, rubber devils showing their tongue, and everything else from that world of wonders thought up for kids and old women, for all those eyes craving color, glitter, and a gaudy excess reminiscent of the flower-strewn interiors of small country churches. And the whole lot was prepared for his arrival, the coming of the Plebeian King.

Because the people loved him like no one else before him. When you drove around the villages and small towns you would see photographs of him everywhere. They'd be displayed in the windows of old wooden houses or stuck in the casements of hundred-year-old cottages; they would fade in the sun, blurring and aging along with him, along with the homes and their inhabitants. Sometimes they'd be mounted in gaudy picture frames from a fair; sometimes they'd be adorned with papal flags made of paper; sometimes they'd hang next to a picture of Our Lady of Częstochowa; but always they would be found in old crumbling dwellings in the kinds of small towns and villages that look as if they're about to disappear off the face of the earth.

With the passage of years his face more and more came to resemble the faces you could see right there in Dukla, or elsewhere in the provinces of Poland. It looked like all the faces to be found at markets, in village inns, at fairs, and in buses leaving county towns for even smaller places. With the passage of time his face became the face of a peasant, the face of a wagon driver. It was as if in old age he were returning to his people. His face was quite unmarked by the stamp of distance, by the alienation or loftiness that inevitably accompanies a rise to power.

Dukla, then, was his kingdom. After all, Wadowice, his birthplace, was only a little bigger. A carnivalesque atmosphere mingled with exaltedness, the smoke of incense with smoke from grilled sausages. On the fringes of the crowd in its Sunday best the local winos deliberated on what to do about the ban on alcohol sales in effect for the day. Mud-spattered hikers came down from the nearby hills with their backpacks, while spotty-faced seminarians stood around in small groups smoking cigarettes concealed in their palms. The town of Dukla, devoid of any houses more than a single story high, lived its great day the best way it knew how.

It was only in the vicinity of the Bernardine monastery, where Mass was to be said, that it was evident something more serious than a big church fair was going on. In places there were beefy guys in special-forces uniforms. They were laden with guns, knives, handcuffs, and walkie-talkies, and in their reflective sunglasses they looked like envoys from some hostile alien world. At the same time, their presence among the old ladies dressed in black and the peasant men squeezed into suits—in the midst of this provincial church throng—bordered on the grotesque. On the roof of the nearby post office snipers were setting up their stations.

I saw him from far off. Dusk was already beginning to fall. His figure was in a circle of light.

He looked frail and lonely. All these people had come here to meet him, but I'd never in my life seen anyone so lonely. The light seized him and imprisoned him like a bird of night. For some reason his arrival had been delayed by several hours and now, while he was still speaking, people were leaving the square in front of the monastery. First individually, then eventually by the dozen, they headed out so they could get home before nightfall. He may have been repeating his famous "Have no fear!" while they were going back to their unmilked cows, unlit stoves, and unfed livestock; or they may just have wanted to take their rest, because they'd been waiting since morning, they'd been on their feet since morning and they were simply exhausted. His aged, trembling voice rose over the town and faded away in the gathering dark.

At that moment it occurred to me that in a few hours everything would fall silent; the people would leave, the cars and buses would drive away, Dukla would be plunged into darkness, and he would remain in a quiet, stark room prepared for him at the monastery. He'd get ready for bed, listening intently to his own body that was growing weaker from day to day. He'd feel a tiredness that could not be overcome by any amount of sleep. I imagined him going up to the window and gazing out into the dark, then turning round and touching the various pieces of furniture—the chairs, the table. Then he'd go to the bed and lie down, overcoming the resistance of his refractory body. I was fascinated by his loneliness and by the moments when he became an ordinary human being. I imagined him waking in the morning when there was no one around. He lowers his feet gently to the floor and feels for his slippers. Then there's the bathroom with its icy, merciless light and the reflection in the mirror over the sink. And as I stood there in Dukla, listening to his great, famous words, I wondered if he shaved alone, staring at his own face in the early morning in the merciless bathroom light—if he repeated this banal action of millions of men all around the world as they get ready to leave for work. That was what occupied my mind—his humanity.

The fact that he was slowly beginning to depart, that he was gradually preparing for that longest of journeys, I learned in a roundabout way. A certain major West European weekly asked me to write a text about the significance of his pontificate. I wrote back: *Pardon*, I'm no hyena. They responded: OK, we understand. Yet I realized then that the countdown had begun, that this time there'd be no miracle as there had been after the assassination attempt. If a major West European weekly is asking for something along the lines of an obituary, it knows what it's doing and no doubt has information from the best sources.

I began to wait for his death. It was one of the strangest feelings I've ever had. I didn't want him to die, but at the same time I knew his death would be essentially a joyful and sublime event—that it would be the fulfillment of a destiny and simultaneously a great test to which our minds and hearts would be put. His great "Have no fear!" was finally to be realized, the poetry and the rhetoric to become reality. I listened to the radio and read the newspapers. I paid attention to his weakening, indistinct voice; I studied photographs of his distressed face and his mortified body. Dear Lord, I felt sorrow and at the same time joy, because he had the courage to show the whole world how a person dies. I kept repeating inside: show us all how to die, show us the fate of a human being; show us greatness of soul mingled with the degradation of the body; show us everything it is to be human.

And now, when it's all over, I have the impression that with his wisdom and his humor he saved his most important lesson for the very end. He left us with his death as if it were an exercise we would have to complete without his help. He bequeathed to us his death, his dying. In this idiotic world where old age has become outlawed, where sickness and weakness border on the criminal, where anyone who lacks the strength to produce and consume becomes an outcast, where failure and destitution are acceptable only in television reports from distant lands, he had the courage to die with millions watching; he had the courage to show us his wasted body, his face constricted with suffering, his dragging feet, his death throes. This was his last lesson, at a time when he could no longer speak.

You don't need to be a Christian, you don't need to be a believer, to comprehend it. This lesson was directed at us as the human community; it told us that no one need suffer and die alone. That the suffering and death of each of us is a concern for us all. The miracle of the birth of humanity was a miracle of the birth of community. These days we gather in herds to play, to stifle our fear, or to fight. When the time comes to die we go off alone. But really we're being removed from sight so as not to spoil the mood of others. Death, which we know will come—and this awareness is what distinguishes us from the animals—has become something like an embarrassing disease. Instead of shaping our lives and giving them meaning, death has been banished to somewhere on the borderline between medicine and horror fiction. And we can once again enjoy our animality, which is supposed to give us a blessed feeling of immortality. But in this we are sorrier and more pathetic than an ordinary dog living its doggy life without fear of what is to come.

Today I heard on the radio that Benedict XVI has issued an irrevocable decree ordering the immediate commencement of the beatification process. This is a beautiful and significant gesture. Yet at the same time—on a relative scale—it's also reminiscent of the febrile mood in Poland. Here the process of beatification has been going on for a long time already. Now it's merely grown stronger. Even before the Pope died, there were about two hundred and thirty statues of him in this country. In April and May several hundred towns proposed raising more monuments. The cheapest one, life-size and made of artificial materials, is to cost four thousand zlotys. A thirteen-foot-high one will cost twelve thousand. In addition to this there are plans to construct gigantic mounds, great gateways, or triumphal arches, as well as figures that will be at least as tall as the Statue of Liberty. Next to such pagan measures, Benedict XVI's decision seems modest, traditional, entirely Christian, and only a little feverish.

Both sainthood and monuments lay waste to his memory. His humanity will disappear, his pain, his simplicity, his white socks and dark red slippers and his Slavic face, which with the passage of years looked more and more like the faces of those who placed his photograph on the windowsills of country cottages. All this will vanish, clad in bronze or lost in the scent of incense. No one should make a saint of him. He should be left in what we call in Polish "saintly peace." He should live on in popular legend as an unofficial, unorthodox saint, who can be prayed to on matters inadmissible for regular saints. Matters that even God himself finds hard to accept. Amen.

Tranquility

In those days, in the villages there were no trash containers. There was also no trash.

People bought all kinds of things, but not much was left after they were consumed. Sugar was sold in paper bags that afterwards could be burned in the stove or reused. Bottles that had contained vinegar, oil, and vodka could be sold back at the store for decent money. They could also be used as containers for homemade cherry juice and raspberry cordial. The special bottles from orangeade and beer that had wire-and-spring mechanisms with a porcelain stopper were utilized to hold homemade carbonated drinks, produced with yeast and sugar. There was hardly any plastic; there were no aluminum-lined cartons. After things were eaten nothing remained.

Animals were slaughtered and consumed. The dog got the bones. The hide could be sold. In those days, leather was expensive. Actually, wool too. People left little behind. Whatever was left could be burned or given to the animals—to the dogs, or to the pigs, which ate anything. There were no trash containers. There was no trash. That I remember.

At the end of the 1960s and the beginning of the 1970s, I spent almost every vacation at my grandparents'. The bus from Warsaw took about three hours. It went east. Inside, it smelled of the country. It was the smell of cleanliness from before the age of deodorants—soap, freshly laundered clothing, mothballs, and human sweat. The women were returning from market. They'd sold their cheeses, cream, and chickens, and now their bodies smelled of it all, of starch and Sunday best. From the driver's seat at the front of the bus came the aroma of dark tobacco, because back then drivers could smoke. No one forbade it. The only thing they couldn't do was talk to the passengers. It was written on a sign in black letters on a white background: no talking with driver. Someone was always sitting underneath the sign—an acquaintance, relative, pal, neighbor—and they'd be chatting up a storm. This other person would sit on the mask of the engine, which looked like an upturned bathtub, and he'd have lit up a cigarette too. The two of them would smoke and talk. At the time I was ten or twelve and I dreamed of sitting there too. It was the best seat on the whole bus—uncomfortable, hot, narrow, with your feet to one side and your neck twisted, and the entire time you had to hold on to a rail or a grip so as not to fall off.

I was ten years old and I was a boy from the city.

My grandparents' house was set back from the road. It was a couple of hundred yards to the nearest neighbor, and three quarters of a mile to the village. My grandparents were often busy working in the fields. I spent long hours alone. The house stood in an old orchard. It was dark and filled with unfamiliar smells. The wooden floors creaked. I walked around on tiptoe, and the creaking followed me from room to room. I was alone, but my solitude in some way kept me company. On the walls, in solid frames, there were religious pictures and my grandparents' wedding photograph. In this way the sacred mingled with the temporal. My grandparents became a little unworldly, while the Virgin Mary was more human. The house seemed large, though it only consisted of two rooms and a kitchen. On the other side of an unlit hallway was a storeroom where Grandfather kept cereal crops. Its wooden partitions were filled with golden wheat and gray-gold rye. The grains were cold and smooth. I would plunge my arms in up to the elbow. I'd remember stories of people who drowned in grain. Maybe not in wheat or rye, but in flax. Apparently it was so slippery that a person would sink into it as though it was water. They'd drop right to the bottom.

Solitude, then. Entire days in quiet and solitude. In the gloom of the old orchard. On pleasant days the sun would penetrate the branches of the apple trees and light up the green shadows. Golden patches of light would create a labyrinth. As you walked slowly along you could feel the successive touches of warmth and cold on your skin. A step or two further and it became brighter and warmer; then a moment later it was shadowy again and there was the dampness of dew, which in places seemed never to dry.

The kitchen window looked out onto the farmyard. The barn, the stable, the pigsty, the summer kitchen known as the *murowaniec*, and the house all formed a square. A handful of slender aged poplars grew in the yard and offered shade; their shadows moved as the day progressed. The rectangle of earth—trodden by cattle, pecked at by hens—became a kind of elaborate sundial. At times, in a patch of bright light a cat, a rooster, or a flock of sparrows would come into view. Then they'd disappear again at the edge of the shadow. It was a little like an irregular chessboard. Things and animals appeared on it then vanished as if they were taking part in an intricate game, the stakes of which were existence itself. I sat in the window and for hours on end I'd observe this slow, almost immobile spectacle. The sundial and the game of chess. In July and August. Almost every year in my late childhood and early youth.

Some things, though, were thrown out. For example pots with holes in them. Nothing could be done with them. They were no good for anything. Some simply broke. In others the bottom burned through. Aluminum wasn't always used in those days. Pots were made of brittle cast iron or low-grade sheet metal that was coated with white enamel but was still vulnerable to corrosion.

On the far side of the summer kitchen there was something like a trash heap. This isn't a good term for the place. Let's say that amid the weeds and nettles there was a sort of cemetery of objects. Though that's not right either, because the objects that lay there weren't entirely dead. True, the pots had ceased to be useful, but they hadn't lost their shape. They still retained the space that they formed, they still contained something, even if it was only indifferent air, dust, or the white shoots of plants sprouting in their sheltered, cracked insides.

The fate of the pots was shared by kerosene lamps that were called *wózowki* or "wagon lamps." They were used as lights on carts as they returned home in the evening. They also came in handy when you were moving around the stable and the barn in the dark. They didn't give a whole lot of light, but their flame would stay lit even in the strongest wind and was relatively safe. Because in those days, in that part of the world, there was still no electricity.

Sometimes in the evening I'd peep into the cattle shed while my grandmother was milking the cows. It was almost completely dark in there. The lamp only provided a faint illumination in its immediate vicinity. It gave light only for itself. I could sense the warmth and the smell of the animals and I could hear their breathing, but I couldn't see anything. Grandmother would be murmuring something to the cows. I heard streams of milk hitting the bottom of the pail. But nothing could be seen. Except that maybe, in the place where the lamp stood, the darkness was a few tones lighter; shadows moved there, a momentary silhouette would appear in the gloom and immediately be swallowed up again. It was a little scary, a little uncanny, and very beautiful. I would stand in the doorway enveloped in the warmth of the cattle and imagine to myself that the night was boundless, that it extended infinitely in space and would last forever. It was easy.

Then I would leave my grandmother alone. She didn't like to have company during the milking. She believed the cows were uneasy when someone else was there. I'd wait for her in the house. After a while she'd emerge from the dimly lit hallway. The milk in the pail was white and unreal. The whiteness was at odds with the dark of night and the black rectangle of the door to the cattle barn. But afterwards, when Grandmother had already strained the milk and I'd been given my regular evening mug, everything would go back to where it belonged. The thick warm drink contained heavy, sleepy animality. It came directly from out there, from the heart of the night filled with the animals' breathing.

The lamps ended up in the bushes with the pots. When I found them they'd already be eaten away with rust. The flame had evidently burned right through them. The metal would fold at the touch like paper. There was no trace whatsoever of the smell of kerosene.

There were also clocks. Ordinary wind-up alarm clocks. They must have been pretty poor quality, since my grandparents kept having to buy new ones and throw the old ones away. Maybe one alarm clock would last a year? Maybe eight thousand seven hundred and sixty hours would gnaw right through the simple spring mechanism? I don't know. It's possible my memory is mixing with my imagination and multiplying the number of discarded clocks. Maybe there were only a handful of them: two, at the most three?

Someone must have dismantled them first, as if curious why they'd suddenly fallen silent and stopped working. Their innards were made of some kind of rustproof alloy, or perhaps they'd been galvanized. In any case they were quite resistant to rain and snow and for a long time they glistened with a yellowish or golden color. These precise and fragile devices looked sad and strange as they lay abandoned amid the nettles and rocks and cast iron fragments. The geometric precision of the high-quality steel coils looked strange in the chaos of the trash heap. I never asked my grandparents about the clocks. I guess I accepted their presence in the brush beyond the summer kitchen as something completely natural. In those days and in that place things and events were entirely natural and at the same time passing strange.

Today I'm aware that the metal alarm clocks were the most complex mechanisms in my grandparents' home. But just like the pots, nothing could be done with them once they fell silent. They became absolutely useless. They measured time and as a result they themselves became a kind of materialized abstraction. In real life there was nothing for them to do. They lay in the nettles being rained on.

Long hours, then, in solitude and quiet. In those days there were many fewer sounds. A couple of times a day a bus would drive by in the distance. You could see its shape on the far highway, moving between two rows of trees. Somewhere a cow lowed. Somewhere a dog barked. Every sound was clear and was distinct from other sounds. Between them there was total silence. It was as if from time to time reality held its breath and lowered its eyelids. From a farm several hundred yards away you could hear the winch of a well turning, the chain unwinding and the bucket descending into the shaft. Sometimes sounds came from very far away indeed. From somewhere beyond the horizon, from the depths of the sky, from goodness knows where. All at once, in the quiet of a still and sweltering afternoon a snippet of someone's conversation would be heard. The vibrant air was like a piano's sounding board or a violin string, and would carry distant human voices, the clatter of tools, the creak of a horse-drawn cart. Yet all around, as far as the eye could see, nothing whatsoever was happening and nothing moved.

On those lonely hot days, when Grandmother and Grandfather were working in the fields, I felt as if I were taking part in someone else's dream.

I'd go into the barn and carefully close the door made of untreated planks. Inside, semi-darkness reigned. The barn had a thatched roof and even on the hottest days it was cool there. Slanted strips of light entered through cracks between the boards of the wall, illuminating golden swirls of dust. As I walked deeper into the shadowy space, over and again I disturbed the trembling planes of light, which reconstituted themselves immediately after I passed. There was a smell of grain and hay. Chickens poked around amid the scattered stalks of straw in search of food. A cat was hunting a mouse. Sparrows perched on the beams up by the roof, waiting for the cat to go away so they could rejoin the chickens.

The handles of the pitchforks were smooth, cold, slippery. I tried to imagine how many times they must have been held in my grandfather's or grandmother's hand for the hazelwood shaft to have acquired such smoothness. A hundred thousand touches? A million? The surface of the wood was soft and had a dull sheen. In fact, it recalled the surface of a human body. This seemed quite natural, since with the passage of time it was less and less a piece of wood, and had come more and more to resemble a person. The same was true of the wooden rakes. If you used them properly they were virtually indestructible. Every once in a while one of their tines would break, but it was easy to replace, a new one whittled down and inserted in the place of the old. For some reason, back then, things lasted much longer. You could say they lasted till death, till death from old age. It's easy to imagine a tool that—from the touch of matter, from its own function—gradually turns into nothingness.

Though actually there was no need to imagine anything. I remember a long knife with an ebonite helve. The blade was over eight inches in length. At one time it had been more than an inch and a quarter wide, but now all that was left was a strip of steel half an inch across. The whetstone, the hone, the file, and everyday use had eaten away at the metal and ground it down, and now this handy village knife looked like an assassin's dagger or a misericord. It would only have been good for administering a mortal thrust. Nevertheless, my grandfather sharpened it obstinately because he believed the steel of the knife was of exceptional quality, and "they don't make them like that anymore." I didn't know how old the knife was. It may well have come from some remote, almost legendary "pre-war" time, when objects were sturdier and were more likely to survive a person than leave him an orphan. And I wouldn't be at all surprised if that knife of my grandfather's had once belonged to his father, my great-grandfather, whom I never knew.

The world was composed of an infinite amount of time and material reality. It barely contained any people or events, ordered according to the rules of dramaturgy. In the shade, on long July days, in the silence, everything happened at the same time. Images were suspended in space, able to last forever. Sometimes they broke from the pressure of the air, but then they reassembled themselves. It seemed to me I could easily return to what had been an hour or even a day or two before. And I believe I did so all the time. Perhaps I even found my former self, busy with whatever had been occupying me earlier?

Today, I have the feeling that back then I was experiencing something like eternity. Exactly that. Grace had been conferred upon me.

At dusk the dew would form and the cows would return from their pasture. Eventually Grandfather let me drive them. At the end of the orchard there was a meadow. The land dipped and then rose. In the middle of the meadow someone had once dug a well. Instead of a well-shaft poking out from the ground there was a framework of decaying green boards. Sometimes the cattle drank there at noon. There was no sweep or hoist. You just needed a long pole with a hook, on which you lowered the bucket. The well basically looked like a natural waterhole that had been indifferently fenced off with rotting planks. Its rim was overgrown with grass. It was as if the earth had voluntarily parted in this place to reveal a cold, greenish eye of water. I was a little afraid of the well. Its presence in the landscape was a provocation. It was nobody's. It didn't belong to any house or farm. No one was its master. That was why I would look fearfully into its depths and sense how flimsy, how temporary the timber was that separated it from the rest of the landscape. Its water was a little cloudy and had a metallic, alien taste.

I would pull up the metal stakes the tethers were attached to and the cows would set off, dragging their chains behind them. Now, from the meadow, the house and orchard and the whole farm looked more imposing. Dusk was falling. The trees and buildings on the rise would be turning black and dissolving into a single shape. Against the backdrop of the darkening sky the farm looked like the entrance to an immense cavern. I would walk behind the cows. Their chains would trail through the cold wet grass with a gentle rattling sound. In the dying glow of day the steel glistened dark blue. The farm loomed closer. Its darkness was going to swallow us up—the cows and I were about to enter it and find shelter for the rest of the night. The cows knew the way. We'd cross the black ring of trees and come to a stop inside the rectangle of buildings. I would unfasten the chains, coil them up and hang them on the wall of the cattle shed. The yard was a little lighter and warmer. The bare trampled earth was giving back the heat it had absorbed during the day. The smell of pigs drifted from the sty and lingered over the farmyard like strands of mist. It was so quiet I could hear the horse shiver in its stable. No one was around. The animals would be resting in their places.

I felt I was alone in the world, and this brought me joy. Beneath the dark night sky, amid the smell of cattle, somewhere at the end of the world, I was more aware of my own existence than ever before or ever again.

Sometimes Grandmother would send me to the store for a loaf of bread.

I'd leave the orchard and enter into open space. The summer was dazzlingly bright. The crops were ripening. A lark would be singing its monotonous, hypnotic song in the sky. The heat, the glare, and the unvarying sound in the absolute stillness. Nothing moved. It was all alive but immutable. I gripped the money in my hand, and as I followed the field boundaries I was certain that nothing would ever change, that what I was seeing and experiencing would remain as it was forever. That I'd be able to come back here in ten years and follow the same track. And even after I died, this scenery, this world, and the undulating line of the horizon would wait for me.

And then my heart would race, because the path led through a stand of old trees that was supposedly a burial ground for cholera victims in the previous century. Amid the thorny undergrowth it was hard to make anything out, but it was common knowledge this was an old cemetery. Everyone said so. I'd hold my breath and quicken my pace. I had the impression that among the brush and the trees it was even quieter and hotter than elsewhere. I'd walk quickly, but nothing could have forced me into a run—I sensed someone's presence behind my back, but I didn't want to let on.

Then the track led between pastures. The first houses of the village could be seen in the distance.

As you entered the village everything became a little grayer. The farmyards were dusty and the dust spilled out onto the edge of the road. The houses stood close together and because of this became less distinct. In those days most of them were wooden-built. The wood had turned dark brown from the sun and rain. Today I can't recall the shape of a single one of them. Instead I remember the spaces between them, those sudden gaps in the line of buildings, the hollow inlets of courtyards, the in-between places, everything that was not "the village itself" but precisely the empty space that gave meaning to the human dwellings.

There was a smell of wood smoke. Usually pine. But you could also smell aspen and poplar. Coal was burned in the winter. In the summer the scent of sap mingled with the kitchen smells. It was the odor of living human households: smoke, heated oil, lard, fried onion, potatoes on the boil, and sometimes meat sizzling in the pan. It was all mixed with the dusty scent of the road and the smell of cattle from the farmyard, from the open stable door and the sties. In the burning space of summer it was absolutely impossible to separate what was human from what was animal. The motionless heat of July melted reality like wax. The world had a semi-liquid, hallucinatory texture. In such stagnant weather a dust devil would sometimes form. It would lift dirt and trash in a spiraling tangle, move down the middle of the road, and vanish into nothingness as abruptly as it had appeared. At such moments old women would cross themselves, because Evil didn't only come at midnight. It could just as easily show up at noon. Scrubbed pots would be drying upside down on fence posts. I was ten years old and I was a boy from the city.

I don't remember people's faces. I don't remember my grandmother's or my grandfather's face. I remember their images captured in old-fashioned photographs. When I try to recall them I have to imagine them. I have to use the force of my will to bring the sepia pictures to life, to make them speak. Yet I spent hours with them, days, weeks. I believe I remember their gestures and their movements. I can see my grandmother sitting on the edge of the bed after a hard day's work;

she folds her hands in her lap, looks through the window into the depths of the twilight, and begins to speak, begins to tell a story that seems unconnected with the present moment. Then Grandfather appears in the door. He pulls up an old footstool that stands by the stove. He climbs up on it and, as usual at that time, he lights the kerosene lamp that hangs from the ceiling. At this moment Grandmother breaks off her tale for a while, stands up, crosses to the white dresser, and takes out plates. She lays them on the table.

When Grandfather's already busy eating, she returns to her place on the bed and resumes her interrupted story. Grandfather doesn't speak. He leans over his plate and eats slowly, solemnly; he eats with dignity, almost religiously, because he belongs to a generation for whom hunger is something commonplace and self-evident.

I was ten years old. I sat by the stove, observing their life. I was a boy from the city and it seemed to me that what I saw would never pass. That may be the reason why these images keep coming back to me, like a recurring dream. Or like an eternity, thanks to which memory can regain its strength and its faith.

———————

ANDRZEJ STASIUK has received numerous awards for his work, including the NIKE, Poland's most prestigious literary prize, for his collection of essays *Going to Babadag.* His 1999 novel *Nine* was recently published in English to great acclaim.

BILL JOHNSTON is the leading translator of Polish literature in the United States. His translation of Tadeusz Różewicz's *new poems* won the 2008 Found in Translation Award and was a finalist for the National Book Critics Circle Poetry Award.

SELECTED DALKEY ARCHIVE PAPERBACKS

FOR A FULL LIST OF PUBLICATIONS, VISIT:
www.dalkeyarchive.com

SELECTED DALKEY ARCHIVE PAPERBACKS

FOR A FULL LIST OF PUBLICATIONS, VISIT:
www.dalkeyarchive.com